REACHING THE PINNACLE

A Methodology of Business Understanding, Technology Planning, and Change
(Implementing and Managing Enterprise Architecture)

By

SAMUEL B HOLCMAN

Pinnacle Business Group, Inc.
Enterprise Architecture Center Of Excellence (EACOE)
Business Architecture Center Of Excellence (BACOE)
Samuel.Holcman@PinnacleBusGrp.com

ISBN: 0615669875

ISBN 13:   9780615669878

Library of Congress Control Number: 2012944343
CreateSpace, North Charleston, SC

Foreword

How does an organization gain an advantage over its competition? I have often heard from people in the information technology community suggest it comes through increased "agility". Contrary to this popular belief, I do not believe that agility necessarily means handcrafting information systems faster and/or smaller. While both fast and small can be helpful – neither of these are the critical component. Agility means being able to react to internal demands, and external opportunities, and threats, faster and less expensively than the competition. Decades of history, outside of the information technology community, have shown, that for an organization to become more flexible (agile), two key elements are required: (1) architecture, and (2) "assemble to order" (building and manufacturing) processes. I have come to believe these are the essential elements of agility for businesses in the future.

I first met Sam Holcman, and the Pinnacle Business Group, Inc. decades ago. When I ran across their work in Enterprise Architecture, I "liked" it (this was well before Facebook), but could not fully figure out why, until I had a one-on-one meeting with Sam in Detroit, Michigan one afternoon. After a few minutes of polite banter, we started talking about backgrounds, my training as a lawyer, and his background as an engineer. I remember grabbing a marker pen, and diagramming the process that lawyers go through, laying out a legal case to a jury. The process involves developing a logical path for the jury to follow, from the initial framing of the essential issues in the case, to creating an understanding of the relevant evidence, which then usually leads to a story that weaves together the critical elements with the relevant laws, and then ideally to a conclusion. This process sometimes involves taking something of significant complexity, describing or breaking it down into bite-size chunks in a manner that people with possibly no direct knowledge of the subject area can understand.

When this is done skillfully by a good lawyer, a jury of average citizens usually can handle cases of enormous complexity and confusing details. On a parallel board, Sam laid out his Enterprise Architecture process. The legal process I described, and the Enterprise Architecture process he described, were startlingly similar. Smiles came to both of our faces!

This book is about architecture – enterprise architecture. Be careful to not confuse this with enterprise *IT* architecture commonly discussed within a CIO's organization; this is about true, business-driven *enterprise* architecture. Enterprise Architecture is like a blueprint, explicitly representing the business opportunities, needs, and desires, and the transformations of these opportunities into solutions, *some of which* are technology-based. It is about understanding something very complex (the Enterprise), describing it in a manner that is both understandable to the business and the technologists (laying out the case), and developing a set of move ahead initiatives (projects) to move the Enterprise to its desired state (the conclusion).

The concepts Sam Holcman, the Pinnacle Business Group, Inc. and its subsidiaries present in this book deserve consideration. This is a book of action, not surveys or choices – moving from theory to implementation. The book offers a no-nonsense, direct, and easy to follow approach to Enterprise Architecture. The Enterprise Architecture process presented is both theoretically sound and actual-practice refined. Nothing is wasted – no "architecture for architectures" sake, just architecture for helping the business run better. Enterprise Architecture is clearly presented as a forward looking process dealing with enterprise issues - not a cumbersome process that generates lots of documentations that nobody reads. I believe that the clear approach presented in this book will increase the likelihood that you will produce an understandable and usable Enterprise Architecture – from both a business and technology perspective.

As Sam often says, Enterprise Architecture is about understanding complexity – enterprise complexity. Your Enterprise is complex – the methodology to understand it should not be!

Let me close with a quote that is attributable to both Albert Einstein, and E. F. Schumacher:

> "Any intelligent fool can make things bigger, more complex, and more violent. It takes a touch of genius – and a lot of courage – to move in the opposite direction."

This book is moving Enterprise Architecture in the opposite direction (the right direction)!

My best as you pursue your Enterprise Architecture development and implementation efforts.

Tony Scott
Corporate VP and CIO
Microsoft Corporation

On Reaching the Pinnacle

My first experience with Enterprise Architecture was influential to many aspects of my career. I had the opportunity to work with the book's author, Sam Holcman, as he not only taught my team about EA, but also worked with us in the practical application of the principles. I used EA as the cornerstone in developing a business and IT strategy for the company I was working for. We were able to take the concepts and apply them at all levels of the organization using Pinnacle's EA methodology, in order to define and align the company strategy for the next 5 years. Beyond that initial experience, I've found many practical uses for an "architected" type of thinking and approach to leading teams, organizing efforts, explaining problems, and creating solutions. I can honestly say that because of my initial attendance in Sam Holcman's EA training class and one-on-one work with him, my career and my capabilities to positively impact the company I work for have both been enhanced greatly.

Ed Rybicki
Director, Process Integration
Information Technology Process and Organization
Volkswagen

This book hits all of the relevant topics for implementing and managing Enterprise Architecture need by the modern EA professional. The coverage of the Pinnacle Business Group, Inc / EACOE methodology for business understanding, technology planning, and change is excellent – a much needed component in the toolkit of today's EA professional.

Brian H. Cameron, Ph.D.
Executive Director, Center for Enterprise Architecture, Penn State University
Founding President, Federation for Enterprise Architecture Professional
Organizations

The Enterprise Framework ™ in reality!
Through the years as an IT professional, I have seen strategies of IT
departments focus primarily on cost reductions activities. The focus or
trend of a non-revenue generating operation (as IT is viewed) is to deliver
and support IT at lower operational costs. The big contradiction is that IT
is still expected to provide the same services, preferable at improved quality
(better) and at greater speed to market (faster). The focus is on the task or
project, not on what makes up the Enterprise.

Technology is an enabler of the business's strategy. It is intertwined with
the Enterprise's operations. In most cases the impact of decisions made
within one department or business function is not well understood across
the Enterprise. Adding two more floors to your house will not work well
without knowing if the foundation of the house can support it. In IT, we
add and remove floors all the time without understanding the overall impact
to the Enterprise. Only through established blueprints of the architecture
and proper engineering will you know the impact of the planned action.
How many Enterprise "blueprints" equals the blueprint of a house?

The reason large centralized business applications, data center consolidations
and outsourcing of services do not provide the expected savings and
becomes challenging to manage, is because of the lack of knowledge of
the overall picture. These are projects that often are initiated to save costs
and improve operations. They are isolated initiatives that make sense on
paper. Everybody do these things so we should do them too. They might
make complete sense. However, without knowing "why the Enterprise do
what they do, how do we do what we do, or need to do, what things are of
interest to us, who is of interest to us, where are the locations of interest to
us and when are we required to do what we do" we are making decisions
in the dark.

The Enterprise Framework represents a shift in thinking. To me it was one of those "light bulb" moments where you realize this is the way to do it. The Enterprise Framework isn't difficult to understand, it is not difficult to practice and it is cheap! No need to make expensive investment in software to be able to apply it to your organization or processes. The challenge is to get people to see the simplicity and be willing to change how we have been doing it for years. Henry Ford represented a shift in thinking for how to build cars. While all other manufactures were doing custom made cars, Ford revolutionized the manufacturing process through building one car for everybody. A different approach but made completely sense. The Enterprise Framework works the same way.

Jon Myklebust
MIS Business Intelligence and Data Warehousing Competency
Warner Brothers Entertainment Inc.

I have had the pleasure of working with Sam Holcman and the Pinnacle Business Group, Inc. both as a student in one of his classes and partnering with him to launch an EA effort using the Quick Start methodology. Sam brings his wealth of practical experience using the concepts of John Zachman's work, and elaborations of Zachman's work in the Enterprise Framework ™, to provide a repeatable process to initiate an EA program. The pragmatic approach laid out in this book enables the practitioner to rapidly develop a thorough understanding and explicit descriptions of organizations in a way that both business and technical resources can easily digest (and collaborate to refine). This gives visibility to opportunities for rationalization and simplification across the enterprise, and ultimately provides a business-driven answer to the all-important question "what do we do tomorrow?" (and next month, and next year) to achieve the organization's future state goals. Turning sound theory into executable practice, Sam provides a straightforward path for using EA to drive value for the organization.

Jeffery A Gades
Manager, Enterprise Architecture

Practicing Enterprise Architecture can be the most exciting, innovative, and rewarding group in the organization. Unfortunately, it can also be the most frustrating, irrelevant and unsuccessful group as well. Over the past 15 years, I have seen patterns that will predict ultimate success or failure of the EA group. Whether your organization realizes it or not, you have a functioning Enterprise Architecture...the key to success is the degree of documenting the architecture, changing the architecture and using a process to manage the architecture. But not just any process- the process must be a highly visible business facing process that enables corporate strategy.

I have personally utilized Sam's approach to EA during my career as a practicing EA professional. Sam's process provides practitioners with a clear and actionable planning process utilizing the Enterprise Framework. At several large organizations I've been a part of, this methodology allowed us to clearly define the as-is and three year to-be architecture that was driven by business strategy. Sam's Quick Start Methodology uses the Enterprise Framework, helping you understand which cells to focus your efforts on. Best of luck!

Mike Boeselager
Lead Enterprise Architect
Briggs and Stratton

I am very happy to finally see Sam Holcman's long-awaited book in print. Written by a practitioner, for practitioners, "Reaching the Pinnacle" is the distillation of Sam's many years of experience in training enterprise Architecture professionals. The book is solidly grounded in the Zachman framework and the Enterprise Architecture Center of Excellence (EACOE) Quick Start methodology, and every chapter of the book relates to that framework and methodology. Enterprise Architecture is clearly presented as more than just an information technology issue of concern to the CIO, but is instead a tool to facilitate business understanding, strategic planning, and alignment of resources toward the goals of a business.

Dr. Robert A. Walker
Director, School of Digital Sciences
Kent State University

Contents

CHAPTER 1

INTRODUCTION

Overview

This book will guide your efforts to improve the effectiveness and efficiency of your organization. It helps business and information technology (IT) professionals and students understand why information planning is a component of business planning, and why information planning requires business participation and, especially, leadership. The detailed sections of this book help business and IT professionals and students understand what Enterprise Architecture is, how to improve the success rate of Enterprise Architecture projects, how to increase the rate of return on all business investments—including IT—and how to deliver an Enterprise Architecture within two to seven months. The planning techniques outlined in this book have also been successfully used for business planning: they are universally effective techniques, regardless of planning domain. Enterprise Architecture is not just about information technology—in fact, it never has been, from our perspective. Enterprise Architecture is about understanding and representing the Enterprise in a manner the business community understands, and it communicates this understanding to technology personnel for automation and mechanization where desired. Yet, Enterprise

Architecture can serve the business community independent of automation or technology implementation. It allows more precise, less ambiguous, and more consistent communication between business personnel, and also between business and technology personnel.

Strategic Planning

In the 1970s and 1980s, the concept of business "strategy" gained a foothold in the United States. Michael Porter and Peter Drucker spearheaded much of the thinking in this direction. This was about the time the Japanese became known for their manufacturing prowess. Japan's ability to mass-produce improved automobiles and electronics impressed the world and overshadowed some of Porter's and Drucker's work.

Information strategy became an academic topic. Although IT professionals would pay lip service to strategic planning, unfortunately its implementation in the field was "full speed ahead, direction optional." (Yes, I was one of these!) As a result, information technology costs spiraled out of control. Most organizations were spending over 70 percent of their technology budgets on maintenance and support (and unfortunately, as of the writing of this book, still do.)[1] This left little room for strategic projects, investing in new technologies, and keeping up with the rate of business change. Rather than using a business-driven, strategic approach to budgeting, most technology organizations created their budgets using a bottom-up, technology-focused approach. Managers were asked to estimate their funding requirements, and while some managers contacted colleagues, vendors, and industry experts regarding new innovations and industry trends, others anticipated demand based on pending change requests by communicating with other business partners. These disparate approaches resulted in stove pipes of technology, redundant systems, and overlapping functionality. Information technology organizations grew while the backlog of requests for automation increased. Business managers were generally, and understandably, not happy with the overall quality of service from their technology organizations. Thus, many business managers created shadow technology organizations to meet their needs as the centralized technology backlog grew. This resulted in additional stovepipes and a growing legacy of systems.

What is the objective of Enterprise Architecture?

In the context of Enterprise Architecture, *enterprise* refers to a collection of organizations or people with a common set of goals and a single bottom line. *Enterprise* can refer to something as large and complex as all the nations in the United Nations. It can also refer to a small, private company or a division or department within a company. An enterprise can be a corporation, a business unit, a government organization, a department, a program, a project, or a network linked by a common objective.

In the same context, *architecture* refers to the art and science of designing and building something (generally of significant complexity), and the manner in which components and artifacts are organized. In this book, the full definition of Enterprise Architecture is:

> *the practice of explicitly describing an organization through a set of independent, non-redundant artifacts, defining how these artifacts interrelate with each other, and developing a set of prioritized, aligned initiatives and roadmaps to create an understanding of the organization, communicate it to stakeholders, and move the organization forward to its desired state.*

The objective of Enterprise Architecture is to facilitate business understanding, technology and strategic planning, and alignment of information technology with business needs. Technology is now integral to every enterprise, and technology strategic planning cannot be done in a vacuum. Technology strategic planning requires enterprise direction. Enterprise Architecture is the art and science of designing and building a series of representations—*artifacts*—that describe the business area under analysis in a clear and understandable way to the many key people involved in the Enterprise: both business and technology personnel.

> *Enterprise Architecture artifacts can describe strategies, business drivers, principles, stakeholders, units, locations, budgets, process, processes, services, information, communications, applications, systems, infrastructure, etc.*

Business and technology executives use Enterprise Architecture to discover and plan projects that improve the business, may result in technology initiatives, and are required to meet the organization's long-term business goals. Enterprise Architecture's primary focus is on business and business improvement, and its secondary focus is on technology. It is the job of the

Chief Information Officer (CIO) to assist in improving business results, not just to run and maintain information systems. In today's enterprise, if the CIO believes his or her job is to run and maintain systems, "CIO" should stand for Career Is Over!

Thousands of organizations have launched Enterprise Architecture projects. Some of them introduced improvements that enabled them to achieve very aggressive goals, but most of their successes have been limited to technology standardization because organizations generally lack an understanding of what Enterprise Architecture actually can deliver. Strategic planning requires making tough choices. Instead of being decisive and aligning information technology projects directly with business objectives, most technology departments try to make everyone happy and continue to make changes with little regard for integration, reducing time to market, reuse, or measurable business results.

Why do Enterprise Architecture projects fail?

Enterprise Architecture projects suffer when they are implemented using the wrong approach and the wrong resources. The results are lack of acceptance, lack of understanding, lack of support, and lost opportunities. Applying proven methodologies and techniques from disciplines outside of information technology can help ensure success.

Enterprise architects need to understand both business and technology. They also need a balanced approach to strategic planning that provides a near-term return on investment (ROI) while recognizing long-term benefits. The resulting architecture needs to define a series of initiatives, programs, and projects that improve the organization's long-term strategic position. It is ironic that most people trying to do Enterprise Architecture were trained to fix technology problems. They may even be the organization's best firefighters. So why is it surprising that these information technology people grapple with the idea of strategic planning for years without really knowing what to deliver?

Most industries have separated the concepts of architecture and implementation. Products are designed in product development groups, manufactured in manufacturing facilities, and fixed by people who specialize in repair. The same is true for buildings and planned communities. There are architects, people who specialize in construction, and maintenance personnel. Each role has a different set of requirements around education, training, and experience. Would you take someone from an automobile assembly line and have him or her design the next car? Perhaps, but even if the assembly technician had the right education, he or she may not have the right experience or mind-set. Likewise, not all IT professionals are automatically qualified to meet the needs of information technology planning (Enterprise Architecture).

Enterprise Architecture projects also fail due to lack of planning, time, and/or money. The bigger and more complex the enterprise, the longer it takes to get one's arms around it. Yet, all IT professionals know that time is money and that their business partner needs something now. Which of the following flow diagrams best represents the approach taken in most IT departments?

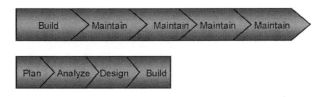

Figure 1.1 – Typical Approach vs. Architecture Approach

Some technology departments take the second approach for targeted technology implementations. However, most technology organizations, unfortunately, take the first approach at the enterprise level. The magnitude of an organization's reliance on this approach can be recognized from its use of such terms as "Version 2," and so on, or from the size of its technology maintenance budget. Do not confuse a need for maintenance with getting it wrong in the first place! However, we forget that if IT does a good job of developing a consistent architecture for the enterprise, it would spend far less time and money fixing things later. Enterprises are very complex. They can support multiple business units, products, customers, employees, locations, processes, and systems around the world. Yet, people continually change their enterprises without understanding the impact of individual changes, the effect of one change on another, or the cumulative effect of all the changes. When you build a balsa-wood model airplane, you do not need much architecture. When you build an airplane capable of carrying three hundred people across the ocean, you need architecture. When you build a log cabin, you do not need much architecture. When you build a one-hundred-story building, you need architecture. When you have one retail store, you probably do not need much architecture. When you have a worldwide enterprise, you need architecture. As things get more complex, architecture is the key to understanding and simplification. The common required element in complex, physical-world solutions is architecture. If this is not the case for enterprises as well, what is? "Handcrafting" computer programs smaller or faster will not get you there. Looking outside of enterprises demonstrates historically that the way to address increasing complexity and change is to use architecture. Complexity and change in the enterprise can be addressed through Enterprise Architecture.

Architecture requires a starting point, an ending point, and a transition plan. Some Enterprise Architecture projects create a target architecture or future vision but neglect to understand the current state of the enterprise and to create a transition plan. You must first understand the current state needs, because they are the baseline for managing change and measuring the effects of change. If you do not know where you are, how do you know you are headed in the right direction? People apply the simple start, end, and transition concepts to their careers, finances, vacations, and even driving; yet some enterprise architects only focus on the target architecture and wonder why it never gets implemented.

Enterprise Architecture requires a *blueprint*: a graphic representation of the models and textual representations that describe the current enterprise, target architecture, and plan for moving from the current state to the target state. It is very difficult to build a cohesive enterprise or manage the effects of change without a blueprint. It is hard to see the effects of change in a thousand pages of text. Take a cue from the way one-hundred-story buildings are planned: graphical representations are key for understanding complexity.

What can we learn from the architecture of buildings?

According to the *Encyclopedia Britannica*, "Architecture is the art and technique of designing and building, as distinguished from the skills associated with construction." The *Encyclopedia* also states that the practice of architecture emphasizes relationships and support activities. Architecture has been successfully applied to many disciplines. Civil architects design and build structures such as buildings and highways.

Architecture has also been successfully applied to communities, cultures, and the military.

Let's examine the concept of architecture in the context of designing a building. Most people would not build a new home without blueprints. If they are in a hurry to move, they buy or rent a home that already exists. Try to picture a house built for someone who goes to a builder without plans and says, "I just bought this vacation lot. My spouse and I love it because it has so many trees! It is just the two of us. Build me something that is not going to require you to take down trees."

The builder does not ask any questions because he is not into this "architecting stuff." Plus, his client said that the house had to be ready in time for summer—and it is already April! The builder checks out the lot, notes where the trees are, and starts building. The client gets a house that looks like this:

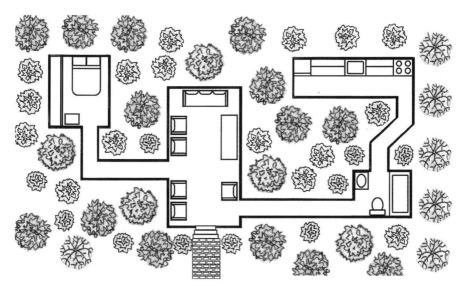

Figure 1.2 – House Built without Architecture

Some people would like this house, but they might wonder why the bathroom is so far from the bedroom. It is easy to demonstrate that you need to architect a home if you want it to meet your immediate and long-term needs. The same is true for the enterprise. It also needs to be designed to a consistent architecture so it can meet long term goals and objectives.

By creating buildings and other physical structures, professionals have learned that there are three general approaches to changing physical things. The first approach is to "go for it" and see what happens. The second approach is to throw it away and start over. Technology professionals have been using both of these approaches for a long time! The third approach is to reengineer something and then change it.

Let's look at the first approach: changing something and seeing what happens. The consequences of "going for it" are high risk, low reliability and learning by trial and error. If the change will not have a significant adverse impact, and it is easy to recover from a failure, "going for it" may be an option. For complex problems, the consequences of this approach can be disastrous.

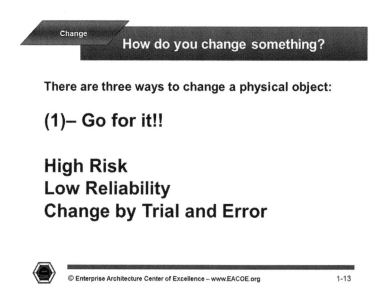

Figure 1.3 – High-Risk Change

Imagine that you need a room that holds a thousand people by the end of the week but that you have one that only holds a hundred. Using the first kind of approach, you could simply move the walls by pushing very hard for twenty feet and then see what happens! If the walls fall in, you dig yourself out and try something else. A lot of enterprise systems fall into this category. Enterprises "go for it" because they do not have anything to base a change on, and because they believe it will take too long to understand the baseline architecture and do a risk assessment and cost-benefit analysis. Someone simply reacts to a change request made by one of their business or technology partners, most often with disastrous consequences. Such changes can rarely be considered truly transparent.

The second approach to change is to throw it away and start over. If we apply this approach to the problem of the too-small room, we might build another room in another building. The existing structure may have exhausted its useful life. We may sell, demolish, or abandon the old building. If we believe someone is still using the building, we continue to maintain it.

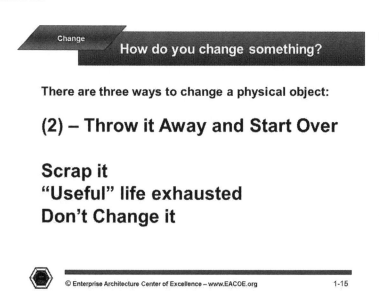

Figure 1.4 – Conservative Change

In some information technology situations, starting over is the best option. For example, if you need to respond to new regulatory requirements, such as Sarbanes-Oxley, and you are running a legacy system with high maintenance costs, replacing the system may be the best option.

Technology departments take the "scrap it" approach because their systems were not designed to a consistent architecture or because they do not have reliable documentation or representation of the present environment. Changeability, flexibility, and scalability are engineering design objectives, not only functions of technology. To change something successfully, it has to be designed to be changed in the first place. When there is no documentation available, or no one who knows the system or application is present any longer, no one wants to break a critical application. So the answer then is "don't touch it," and a new application is built to support the new business requirements. This leads to additional interfaces and escalating support costs, and to more legacy applications.

The third method of change is to "reengineer" something before you change it. How would engineers make a room that holds only a hundred people large enough to support a thousand?

First, they would look for architecture drawings and specifications. Then they would change the drawings. Once the proposed changes were reviewed and approved, they would change the room. If they could not find reliable drawings, engineers would come into the room with drills, tape measures, and probes and then create a representation (architecture) of the current room. Once they have recreated the drawings, they change the drawings. This can be done only because the room was engineered in the first place. They would not change the room until the proposed changes had been reviewed and approved, and the possibility of any unintended consequences addressed.

Change

How do you change something?

There are three ways to change a physical object:

(3) – "Reverse" Engineer and then change it

(Re)create or "find" the Drawings
Change the Drawings
Change the physical object

© Enterprise Architecture Center of Excellence – www.EACOE.org   1-17

Figure 1.5 – Designed Change

The concept of small or transparent changes is not accepted in large, complex engineering projects. Yet we continue to assume that technology changes will not impact downstream process, systems, data, or users. You need Enterprise Architecture to manage change in an enterprise with hundreds or thousands of applications that support a myriad of processes used by thousands of people around the world, and to ensure that the blueprints are created in the first place, documented to support future changes. This can only be done with architecture—Enterprise Architecture. In technology, it is rarely practical to start over, and "going for it" offers too much risk. The third option is generally the best approach.

What can engineering and manufacturing teach us about how to speed up change?

Over decades of practice, the manufacturing industry defined the *manufacturing maturity model*, a three-stage process that organizations mature through as they try to achieve greater flexibility (agility) in their product designs. The three defined stages are *make-to-order*, *provide-from-stock*, and *assemble-to-order*. Assemble-to-order is what allows physical industries to respond to rapid change. However, from a maturity perspective, most information technology organizations (and possibly the overall organization itself) generally operate within the first two stages. Technology professionals have been talking about the third model for well over two decades, but very few organizations have been able to make it work. The answer for would-be agile and flexible enterprises is in front of us if we look outside of the traditional information systems organizations.

Historically, most new developments and activities, as well as manufacturing in the physical world, have begun with a make-to-order approach. When Henry Ford started manufacturing the horseless carriage, it took about six months to make one vehicle since each was built from scratch. The product request began the cycle of development and manufacturing.

This approach naturally results in longer lead times, higher costs, and lower reliability. However, the approach is very common in implementing technology solutions. Information technology organizations start developing a solution to meet vague or assumed requirements. As a result, once something is built and the business "sees" what it is, the mismatch between what the business wanted and what the technologists delivered becomes apparent. Requirements change, the solution takes too long to implement, or it costs too much to rebuild or to maintain. We also generally end up with poor solution quality and resulting data that cannot be integrated—which means that business personnel are unable to get the information they need to make good decisions.

The "Manufacturing Maturity Model"

(1) – Make to Order
Long Lead Times
High Costs
Generally Low Reliability

© Enterprise Architecture Center of Excellence – www.EACOE.org   1-23

Figure 1.6 – Make-to-Order

The next stage in the manufacturing maturity model is *provide-from-stock*. As Henry Ford is supposed to have said of the Model T, "You can have any color you want as long as it is black." In technology, provide-from-stock equates to commercial-off-the-shelf (COTS) application and software packages. Although this approach reduces costs and increases reliability, its tradeoff is limited flexibility. Rather than realize the benefits and inherent limitations of this approach, technology organizations have built an entire industry around customizing, maintaining, "changing," and supporting COTS packages and, in turn, the modifications these organizations have made to the COTS packages—an endless task. Modified COTS packages are actually a case of resorting back to make-to-order: the custom code eroded all of the costs and benefits of the intended solution. Instead of hiring programmers to develop custom applications, we now hire experts in COTS application modifications and maintenance. The net effect is a growing legacy of interface code, and costs that have increased exponentially. We would never think of changing a Buick sedan into a Ford pickup truck, yet we believe that an off-the-shelf payroll package can be turned into an accounting system. Information technology "physics" suggests otherwise.

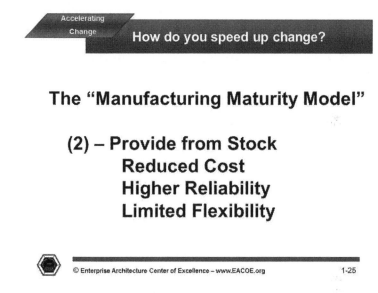

Figure 1.7 – Provide-from-Stock

Assemble-to-order, or mass customization (even in quantities of one), is now common in manufacturing. It uses the concepts of standardized components and deferred differentiation to deliver almost-custom products. This approach affords lower costs, higher quality, high reuse, reduced time to market, and virtually custom products. When you order a computer online, for example, you develop your specification from a list of options, and in a few days you have an almost custom product. You cannot specify a 168 gigabyte (GB) hard drive if it is not on a list of options, but you can specify a 60, 80, or 200 GB hard drive—an almost custom product that comes from the parts list. It will cost you $100 for a 200 GB hard drive. If you really want a 168 GB hard drive, it will cost you $10,000. Why? Because you are now back to make-to-order. This analogy is easy to apply to shopping for hard drives and harder to see in an enterprise, but it has the same order-of-magnitude effect. Most organizations that don't use Enterprise Architecture or assemble-to-order processes in their information technology organizations cannot provide these options in response to business community requests.

Figure 1.8 – Assemble-to-Order

What might the assemble-to-order model look like in your enterprise or its information technology systems? Yes, these concepts can be applied even if your processes are implemented "manually." It is just as important to have assemble-to-order business processes as it is to have assemble-to-order mechanized information systems. This is the key to reuse, reduced time to market, increase in an organization's agility, and coping with the ever-increasing rate of change.

Enterprise Architecture identifies where each of the above approaches should be used within the enterprise. Enterprise Architecture also determines how the enterprise should position itself to take advantage of future innovations. Some of the more specific questions that Enterprise Architecture answers are:

- What steps should we take to position our company for future growth?

- What products should we develop to stay competitive?

- Which markets should we enter or grow to stay competitive?

- Should multiple organizations be performing the same function or processes?

- How can we quickly adapt to new legal and regulatory requirements?

- Are our business units different enough to justify multiple systems and business processes?

Why is Enterprise Architecture important now?

Enterprise Architecture is gaining momentum globally for a number of reasons. The United States government has mandated Enterprise Architecture for federal agencies. Additionally, increasing complexity and accelerating rates of change in business and technology are forcing most businesses to look at their enterprise practices and to question whether traditional approaches can address these challenges—hence the launch of Enterprise Architecture efforts.

The United States government effectively mandated Enterprise Architecture in 1996 with the IT Management Reform Act, nicknamed the "Clinger-Cohen Act." In 1999, the President's IT Advisory Committee (PITAC) concluded that research and development in IT at the federal level was too focused on near-term problems. A House Science Subcommittee Hearing reported:

> ...there has been a pronounced shift in federal funding programs away from long-term high-risk projects toward short-term applied research. When faced with rapidly expanding requirements for IT research and with relatively flat budgets, mission agency managers—understandably and correctly—give priority to short-term needs of their mission. While these decisions by agency managers were in the best interests of their agencies, the sum effect is a potential disaster to the nation. The PITAC believes unless this shift away from fundamental high-risk research is reversed, it will threaten the nation's economic leadership, along with the continued beneficial effects on the health and welfare of its citizens, in the coming decades.[ii]

The annual IT budget for the United States government was forty-five billion dollars at the time and now approaches fifty billion dollars.[iii]

Most of the budget was spent on legacy systems and redundant projects, and the federal agencies' technology activities could not keep up with the rate of change or the rising demand for new functionality. Just as for-profit enterprises do, the United States government suffered from poor-quality applications and systems, an inability to integrate data, and lack of automation for critical functions. The government realized that something had to be done. So, the Office of Management and Budget formally mandated Enterprise Architecture when it passed the Electronic Government Act (E-Gov Act) of 2002.[iv] The E-Gov objectives are to:

> *"enhance the access to and delivery of government information and services" and "bring about improvements in government operations that may include effectiveness, efficiency, service quality, and transformation."[7]*

The E-Gov Act said that:
Enterprise Architecture

(A) means

> *(i)   a strategic information asset base, which defines the mission;*

> *(ii) the information necessary to perform the mission;*

> *(iii)the technologies necessary to perform the mission; and*

> *(iv) transitional processes for implementing new technologies in response to changing mission needs; and*

(B) includes

> *(i)   a current architecture*

> *(ii) a target architecture*

> *(iii)a sequencing plan.*

The E-Gov Act called for a standard framework, but it stopped short of defining one and the methodology that would be used to create, implement, and govern the federal enterprise architecture. Government and nongovernment organizations can use this book's definition of a methodology for using a Framework (such as The Enterprise Framework™ or that designed by John Zachman) to architect their enterprises. Methodologies and Frameworks are not the same things. A Framework is a single frame of reference that is required for Enterprise Architecture and is applicable in any profession, including those other than information technology organizations. A methodology is any one of several possible approaches to Enterprise Architecture: they are approaches to enable a Framework. An enterprise-wide, shared understanding of a Framework must be conveyed, and how it should be used as a frame of reference for developing and implementing an effective Enterprise Architecture must be articulated.

Most enterprises and organizations face the same problems the United States government faced in 2002. They are in a constant state of change, and the rate of change is accelerating. Product life cycles are getting shorter, organizations are operating around the clock, people are collaborating with others from around the world, governments are changing legal and regulatory requirements, and each business partner has different expectations. The traditional methods no longer allow technology departments to keep up. Agilely "handcrafting" information systems faster and/or smaller will not work. It has not worked. Enterprise Architecture and assemble-to-order information systems organizations are required to increase agility, respond to new business requirements, and react to continuously changing demands.

Why do we need explicit representations?

Explicit representations improve communication and provide a baseline for managing change. Key facets of most enterprises have been left vulnerable to interpretation because they have not been explicitly represented. If everyone had the same perspective, we might be able to assume that everyone would interpret everything the same way. But different people have different backgrounds, education, training, goals, and objectives. Unless you are the Borg from Star Trek, you cannot simply publish a mission statement, pronounce a series of principles, announce your goals for the year, and leave the rest to osmosis. The more employees, customers, suppliers, and partners you have, the more interpretations you will have.

Explicit representations improve communication. In an above example, a builder created a home based on implicit ideas. These ideas were only in the minds of the client and builder, and they did not envision the same home. If the builder and client had taken the time to make a blueprint of the client's vision—a graphical representation, based on a frame of reference, where all diagrammatic components are unique and exclusive—and if the builder had come back with actual house plans, they would both have saved time, money, and frustration. The most significant benefits that come from explicit representations are the abilities to change rapidly, to save time, and to save money. This is true for physical objects such as buildings, and for complex objects such as multinational corporations. Enterprise Architecture, as defined here, provides for a mechanism to reduce unintended consequences and to analyze changes prior to implementing costly ones.

Why do explicit representations need to be integrated and consistent?

Executives do not have the tools they need to properly evaluate and manage change if they don't have representations that convey relationships between business units, organizations, goals, and process. So they tend to change something when there is need or perceived need. The more issues an executive needs to address, the more changes he or she attempts, unfortunately without a mechanism to evaluate the possible positive or negative results (unintended consequences) of the change. An executive may decide to remodel a building, relocate an office, sell a business unit, or buy a company. What if the best thing to do is to stay the course or find safe harbor and wait it out? Some CEOs and business personnel "hack and slash" to show they are taking action. They do this because they have no choice and do not have the information they need to make good decisions. People simply have not had the right tools to make truly informed and traceable decisions—until now.

Having explicit representations of enterprise components such as organizations, goals, processes, materials, and assets is part of understanding an enterprise. You also need to understand the relationships between these components. Without understanding the relationships between components, it is as if you have all the parts for a product but don't know how to assemble it. Some technology departments architect "point" solutions—solutions for a given issue or requirement. However, they are unable to realize the full benefits of an integrated architecture because they do not understand the relationships between the point solutions they have developed. Today, most large businesses have thousands of applications, not counting the desktop applications (hidden IT) that sometimes actually run the business. Web services, service-oriented architectures, outsourcing (and all the other alphabet-soup technologies), government regulations, mergers and acquisitions, and disparate solutions are making Enterprise Architecture critical.

We must remember that all organizations have an "Enterprise Architecture" whether they have written it down or not. As a matter of fact, if it is not written down, each person has his or her own picture of what the enterprise looks like—the representations are implicit. Enterprise Architecture is about developing a series of *explicit* representations that are understood by planners, executives, businesspeople, and technologists. Enterprise Architecture is about reducing risk and time to market while increasing flexibility and agility and addressing change.

Why do we need one frame of reference (a Framework)?

Organizations are adding complexity by mapping different frameworks, languages, and notations to an environment that is already too complex to understand. Imagine the complexity that is introduced with a corporate merger or acquisition. Business analysts and technology architects should focus on tasks that add business value rather than create additional complexity.

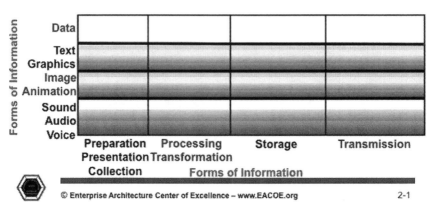

Figure 1.9 – Concepts of Frameworks

To make explicit representations easier to understand, the organization should work with a consistent set of diagrams and symbols that everyone understands. Based on the work of John Zachman and John Sowa from IBM and elaborations thereof, The Enterprise Framework leverages artifacts, diagrams, and abstractions widely recognized by business and technology professionals. To complement The Enterprise Framework, the Pinnacle Business Group, Inc.–Enterprise Architecture Center Of Excellence (EACOE) Enterprise Architecture Quick Start Methodology outlined in this book includes a standard set of diagrams, definitions, examples, and tools for each step in the process of developing an Enterprise Architecture based on The Enterprise Framework. It is important to realize that without these standardized representations, businesses are running off individualized, personal interpretations and networks. Imagine what it would be like if every organization had its own version of the English alphabet—some with sixteen letters, some with twenty-six, and some with a hundred and forty-three! Communication would be impossible. So it is without a Framework that is universal for Enterprise Architecture. There are many ways (methodologies) to use the Framework, but only a single, definite Framework should be used.

The major value of a blueprint, if it is constructed using a universally understood "language," is that the same meaning is obtained no matter who is interpreting the blueprint. A blueprint's value is severely limited if the author is the only person who can consistently interpret the representation. Using a Framework that everyone understands is imperative, and using a methodology in common for Enterprise Architecture provides organizational simplification.

The Enterprise Framework™

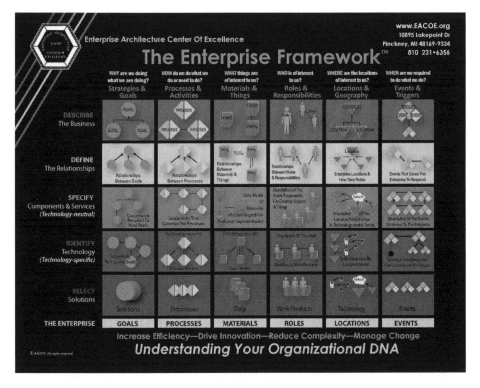

Figure 1.10 – The Enterprise Framework

The first dimension of the Framework contains the six questions (abstractions or interrogatives) that have been used to investigate objects and events for thousands of years. Each interrogative serves a different purpose and is not interchangeable with the others. Each is unique and complete. These investigatory questions are also used in industries such as journalism, engineering, and construction. For example, they are answered at the beginning of any well-written newspaper article. This standard way of exploring things is the first dimension of the Framework. The order of the columns is arbitrary, since the questions do not need to be answered in any specific order. Once a specific order is applied to the Framework columns, a value proposition or methodology is introduced.

Interrogative	Describes
What	Materials/Things
How	Processes/Activities
Where	Locations/Geography
Who	Roles/Responsibilities
When	Events/Triggers
Why	Strategies/Goals

Figure 1.11 – Application of Interrogatives to Business and Information Technology

The second dimension of the Framework indicates the different transformations, and for the most part, possible perspectives, that exist in the enterprise. The transformations are not decompositions. The first row contains the enterprise scope: the goals, strategies, and tactics that describe the business. The second row contains the Business Relationships among the objects in each column, and the third row contains the Technology Neutral View. The fourth row is "Technology Specific" (contains actual technologies), and the fifth row is a representation of solutions specific to each artifact. The last row represents the "Functioning Enterprise." Unlike the columns, the rows have a specific order because they describe quality assurance and governance, ensuring alignment between the business of the enterprise and the information technology enablement of the business.

Each cell at the intersection of a row and column is enterprise-wide in scope, and detail, decomposition, and/or granularity occur within each cell in depth. For example, goals and strategies for the entire organization are contained in the cell at the intersection of Strategies and Goals and the Describe the Business row. The CEO's goals are represented at the "highest" level, and then those goals are stratified into organization and individual goals, as an example.

The Framework identifies everything that needs to be understood about an enterprise; it is the collection of all the perspectives/transformations that represents the functioning enterprise. At the same time, not all thirty architecture views are required before an enterprise gets started. As a matter of fact, most organizations' architectures and strategies can initially be defined by only a handful of cells, as the methodology in this book will show; different types of artifacts will be used in different situations. However, you need to understand that every perspective and transformation is important, and each exists whether or not it is explicitly represented. Having explicit representations for each cell facilitates reuse and makes it possible to associate cells with each other: this is the ultimate in flexibility and agility, and may take some time to effect fully. The associations make it possible to identify gaps and overlaps. Just as not all of the letters of the alphabet are required to make a word or sentence, or not all of the elements in Mendeleev's Periodic Table in are required to make a chemical compound, not all of the cells are required for a given area of analysis in an Enterprise, initially. The Enterprise Framework, when used with an effective methodology, will produce a clear, verifiable, understandable, and effective business and technology strategy. Practitioners have found The Enterprise Framework to be easy to explain and understand. Some have said that "The Enterprise Framework is *human* consumable."

The Pinnacle Business Group, Inc.–EACOE Quick Start Methodology

The Pinnacle Business Group, Inc.–EACOE Quick Start Enterprise Architecture Methodology (aka the Pinnacle Methodology) demystifies the process of designing the architecture of the enterprise. It provides a step-by-step approach to Enterprise Architecture, ensuring the organization meets the goals and objectives established by management. The Methodology enables organizations to use Enterprise Architecture as a decision-making tool for business strategy, information technology development and alignment, risk analysis, and project and program prioritization.

The Pinnacle Methodology includes the processes required to understand the organization's baseline architecture from both a business and technology perspective, to create the target architecture, and to define the transformations that are required to meet the organization's goals. The basic steps of the Pinnacle Methodology are:

1. *Create the target (desired state) architecture.*

   The target architecture includes explicit models that describe the Goals, Processes, Materials (the business objects of IT data), Roles (including organizations), Locations, and Events that comprise the enterprise. It also includes the systems that do or can support the Processes, Materials, and Roles of the organizations.

2. *Identify the baseline architecture.*

   The baseline architecture includes explicit models that describe the Goals, Processes, Materials, Roles, Locations, and Events that presently comprise the enterprise. It also includes the current systems that support the processes and materials of the enterprise.

3. *Analyze the models to identify move-ahead initiatives and their projects, gaps, overlaps, and opportunities.*

4. *Define and prioritize the business and technology initiatives and projects that are required to transform and move the enterprise from its current state to its desired state.*

5. *Partner with business and technology teams to conduct additional analysis ensuring that the projects continue to be aligned with the target Goals and architecture.*

6. *Leverage existing governance structures to guide and advise the target architecture implementation.*

7. *Institutionalize ongoing planning.*

To address issues with resultant quality, involvement, and acceptance, the Pinnacle Methodology makes certain that the correct stakeholders are participating at the right times. As one example of quality assurance, the Pinnacle Methodology ensures that the business strategy and Goals are understood before engaging technology implementation specialists.

The Pinnacle Methodology can be applied to the entire enterprise, a business unit, a department, a function, or a strategic project. The broader the scope of the Enterprise Architecture project, the more likely the organization is to reap the benefits of Enterprise Architecture: integration, reuse, agility, and cost efficiencies. The Methodology can be used in all of its robustness, or it can be treated as a set of tools. If an organization chooses not to represent the whole enterprise, it needs to make informed decisions about which parts of the organization it is initially going to focus on. It also needs to understand why it is focusing on those organization units, and the impact of not focusing on the other units.

The organization needs to define the scope of the Enterprise Architecture project. If the enterprise does not apply the Methodology to a real business situation, the enterprise will simply not gain real business value. The enterprise architects will merely be performing an academic exercise; the technology organization will continue with business as usual.

The project team has not fully applied the Pinnacle Methodology until it understands the relationships and dependencies between models and components within the Enterprise Architecture. For example, the team may have described the Processes the business performs. If the Processes are not aligned with corporate Goals, the employees responsible for those Processes may be wasting resources and confusing stakeholders. Once you have explicit representations and understand the relationships between these "independent" factors and artifacts, you then have the basis for testing your ideas and analyzing the effects of change and for developing the second set of models required for Enterprise Architecture: Implementation Models.

How do we know the Pinnacle Methodology works?

An Example Case Study

The CEO of a large company set very aggressive targets for a segment of its business market. The person responsible for business planning and strategy launched a two-month proof of concept (a prototype) to demonstrate the effectiveness of the Pinnacle Methodology.

The proof of concept was executed by a small team using public information about one of the divisions within the enterprise. The results of the prototype were used to explain the Pinnacle Methodology to the CEO. The CEO supported the approach, and it was then used to develop the strategy and roadmap that enabled the CEO to reach the enterprise goals. This Enterprise Architecture project was so successful that it became a case study used by a major business school.

Summary

Why can you upgrade software on your personal computer faster than you can upgrade a production system at a large, multinational corporation? It's because of the differences in knowledge, motivation, scheduling, and complexity. Your personal computer supports you, and you probably know more about it than anyone else. Since you need it to get your work done, you are not likely to install new software when you have a deadline to achieve. You also have an incentive to fix it when it is broken. Your personal computer is considerably less complex than a production enterprise system. It does not support thousands of people around the world performing different process with different schedules, languages, and deadlines. Additionally, you do not have processes, programmers, and data center personnel continuously making changes to the underlying infrastructure, data, and interfaces. Multiply the complexity in the above illustration by a thousand, and you start to approach the complexity of a multinational corporation or government agency.

Architecture becomes more important as complexity and the rate of change increase. Enterprises are very complex and the rate of change is increasing exponentially. It is fairly easy to identify bad decisions when you look at corporate track records, longevity, and stock fluctuations. Yet, executives and managers continue to shorten their company's life span by "shooting from the hip," creating complex, inflexible enterprises. They don't do it deliberately; they do it because no truly good decision-making tools are available to them. Blueprints and change processes are required to create a complex physical object and maintain the object's relevance in the marketplace. Why would managing an enterprise require anything less?

The Pinnacle Methodology enables organizations to quickly and cost-effectively develop the Enterprise Architecture, provide a platform to anticipate and manage change, analyze the effects of proposed changes, and measure the effects of change. The next chapter provides a more detailed overview of the Pinnacle Methodology. There we discuss inputs, processes, outputs, and roles and responsibilities, along with suggested practices and common issues that may arise.

Over decades of actual practice, we have learned that this Methodology and approach can be used to describe any component of the enterprise from most any perspective. We also learned that different levels of detail are required in different situations. Over the last thirty years, the term *Enterprise Architecture* has been used to refer to individual components of the Enterprise Architecture. For instance, some people refer to the IT infrastructure and technical platforms as the Enterprise Architecture. However, Enterprise Architecture is not only IT infrastructure and technical platforms; it must reflect the entire enterprise itself. A true Enterprise Architecture provides descriptive representations of the business and of the ways technology will best enable that business strategy. Enterprise Architecture is about the enterprise, first and foremost.

The Pinnacle Methodology uses a business-driven approach to define the Enterprise Architecture. The architecture is composed of the Goals, Processes, Materials, Roles, Locations, and Events that describe the enterprise, the future vision, and the projects and initiatives required to implement the future vision.

Note: To avoid confusing readers who have different perspectives, the remainder of the text refers to using the Pinnacle Methodology to develop the Enterprise Architecture as an enterprise architecture planning project.

We define Enterprise Architecture in two ways:

From an information and technology perspective, Enterprise Architecture is explicitly describing an organization through a set of independent, non-redundant artifacts, defining how these artifacts interrelate with each other, and developing a set of prioritized, aligned initiatives and roadmaps to understand the organization, communicate this understanding to stakeholders, and move the organization forward to its desired state.

From a business perspective, Enterprise Architecture illuminates how an organization and all of its members can achieve its objectives through the creation of a series of engineered models and project initiatives that can be easily understood by all of the people associated with the organization.

CHAPTER 2

THE SIX PHASES

Overview

Defining and implementing the Enterprise Architecture will improve the operating efficiency and success of the organization. Enterprise Architecture requires commitment to result in sustained, long-term success—as does any strategy. It will take two to four months to develop an initial architecture, and it may take a few years to transform the organization.

The overarching objectives of an Enterprise Architecture project are to:

- Develop a high-level consensus of the future business vision in terms of objectives, Process, Materials, and information technology assets

- Determine the level and quality of the automation that presently supports the organization's Process and Materials

- Identify and prioritize the projects or initiatives required to meet the organization's Goals and objectives

- Provide an effective vehicle for transforming the organization, managing change, and measuring the effects of change.

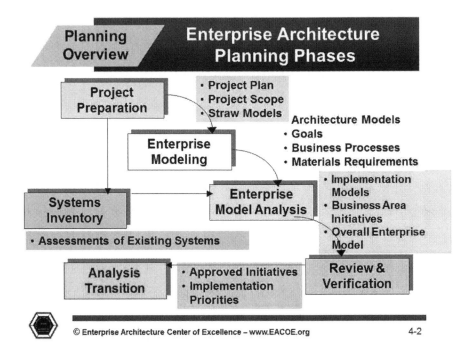

Figure 2.1 – Six Enterprise Architecture Planning Phases

Where does the Pinnacle Methodology work well?

The Pinnacle Methodology has been proven in very large, complex organizations. It has also been successfully used by large, medium, and small organizations. The largest effort was at a Fortune 5 company. The smallest documented effort belonged to a person who woke up one day and said, "I have a five-million-dollar distribution company, but I have no idea how I built it…that makes me very nervous." This was a very intelligent person. After working hard and starting a successful business, he took the time to figure out what was going on and what he should do next. After using the Pinnacle Methodology, his company continues to grow today.

Executive Sponsorship

Aside from execution, an important factor in determining the success of an enterprise architecture planning project is executive sponsorship. The Executive Sponsor is responsible for working with the Project Lead to ensure that all program and project prerequisites are met. After the project is underway, the Executive Sponsor advocates for the project in public and private forums and works with executive management to resolve issues escalated by the project team. An Enterprise Architecture can be developed without executive sponsorship, but sponsorship does make it easier. Given the choice of developing an Enterprise Architecture without executive sponsorship or waiting for executive sponsorship before proceeding, the choice is clear: proceed!

The suggested Enterprise Architecture program and project prerequisites are that:

1. *The Enterprise Architecture project has a high priority.*

    - Action Item: Secure proper top-level executive consensus for the high priority of the effort, minimally across the areas of the business under consideration for this iteration of the Enterprise Architecture development.

2. *Business and information technology management understand the need for enterprise architecture planning, and they support the process.*

    - Action Item: Present educational sessions, workshops, and supporting reference materials that enable all levels of management to find a common understanding of their objectives, challenges, and opportunities in developing the Enterprise Architecture.

3. *The appropriate resources are assigned to the project at the right time. Resources include funding, people, facilities, and equipment.*

    - Action Item: Secure commitment from the proper highly placed people and for the necessary facilities (including several project-only work areas or conference rooms), and support funding for training and other related organizational enablers to stabilize the foundation for success.

4. *The initial enterprise architecture planning project has an achievable scope, and management allocates reasonable, adequate time to complete the project.*

- Action Items: Set up educational sessions to help decision makers to select a starting candidate project scope and to establish a reasonable timetable for the initial projects. Ensure that the Enterprise Architecture teams are adequately prepared with education and discussion of the scope to avoid situations where anyone feels a need to shortcut or not to fully address the required components of a successful project. (Anyone who has prior education in the Pinnacle Methodology can provide excellent input to the management teams as they select the project scope and inherent timeline requirements.)

We use the term "project" to describe this effort here to provide constrained time and focus, although Enterprise Architecture continues until the enterprise no longer exists. Enterprise Architecture projects have a beginning, middle, and end. Enterprise Architecture is continuous. Enterprise Architecture *precedes* enterprise change. It is not "documentation."

If the prerequisites have not been met, the architecture team can build credibility and momentum by gathering existing materials, developing explicit Enterprise Architecture Models and representations, and getting feedback from key stakeholders. Architecture is important for any size application or organization; even grassroots efforts can successfully employ Enterprise Architecture for individual information technology applications or for business transformation and enhancement efforts.

To be successful, an organization should begin with one enterprise architecture planning project that has organizational priority. "Horse races"—competing projects with the same end goal—can be a successful way to breed innovation in various environments, such as product development. However, a horse race (or the perception of one) between the planning project, architecture organizations, and information management groups will undermine enterprise integration and alignment. Your business and technology partners will be confused and will disengage when these groups compete for resources and visibility. The net effect is that your organization will have thrown away a lot of money and squandered an incredible Enterprise Architecture opportunity because of multiple initial approaches and efforts.

Business and information technology leadership must support the effort to integrate the enterprise and thus to reap all the benefits of Enterprise Architecture. Additionally, Enterprise Architecture planning projects generally identify the need for some form of organizational change. Existing staff members may resist change because they are accustomed to the status quo. Business and information technology leadership can mitigate resistance by communicating the importance of the Enterprise Architecture planning project. Executives should proactively address issues regarding motivation, resource allocation, and project participation by creating management objectives and individual goals. As the phrase goes, you get what you measure.

The Enterprise Architecture Project Lead needs to seriously consider his or her own requirements and to let the Executive Sponsor know what is needed to be successful. If the sponsor is unwilling or unable to provide the level of support required, the Project Lead may need to look for a different sponsor. An alternative is to reduce the project scope to something that can be successful within the constraints of the defined sponsorship and funding.

Project Scope

Proof of Concept

The first step in the project is to define its scope as it is formally kicked off. Ideally, the scope is the entire enterprise. However, the initial scope of the project may need to be limited or a proof of concept may need to be carried out to gain additional executive support or to demystify what Enterprise Architecture really is. The objective of a proof of concept is to prove that an idea is feasible and productive and to provide greater understanding of what Enterprise Architecture will provide to everyone involved. Proofs of concept should be conducted in a streamlined fashion with minimal time and resources. The proof of concept should not be treated like a full-scale Enterprise Architecture planning project with rigorous processes and full business participation. Neither should the team and program sponsors forget that it is only a proof of concept and that the resulting business and technology strategy is not intended for implementation. To determine if Enterprise Architecture would have improved the current situation, the team may consider using historical data and compare the resulting architecture and projects to what was actually done.

Defining the Enterprise

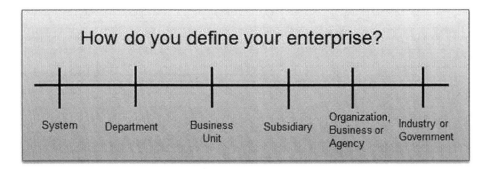

Figure 2.2 – Scale of an Enterprise

In the case of a multinational corporation, the Enterprise Architecture planning project may include all business units and organizations that comprise the company. Subsidiaries of a multinational corporation can be treated as separate enterprises. Which outsourced processes to include in the scope of the enterprise is determined by type of outsourcing agreement. Standard interfaces will need to be defined for organizations, process, materials, and systems that are excluded from the Enterprise Architecture. In the case of a not-for-profit organization or government agency, the Enterprise Architecture should standardize core components and interfaces across the businesses that comprise the organization.

The Executive Sponsor will advise on how the enterprise is defined and will set the scope of the Enterprise Architecture planning project. The narrower the scope, the harder it will be to achieve the cost reductions and quality improvements that are associated with an integrated enterprise, though through follow-on EA iterations, these full opportunities for reductions and improvements are within reach. Achieving initial success is important whether you are an employee or a consultant, so make sure the initial project scope is achievable given the project constraints.

The Six Phases

The Enterprise Architecture planning project is initiated by an Executive Sponsor and a Project Lead. It is started after the scope is approved and the project is funded. The following illustration shows the major inputs and outputs to each phase of the Enterprise Architecture planning project. The diagram is followed by a brief description of each phase. We discuss in subsequent chapters the detailed processes required to complete the deliverables for each of the phases, along with roles and responsibilities for the phases, suggested practices, templates, and examples.

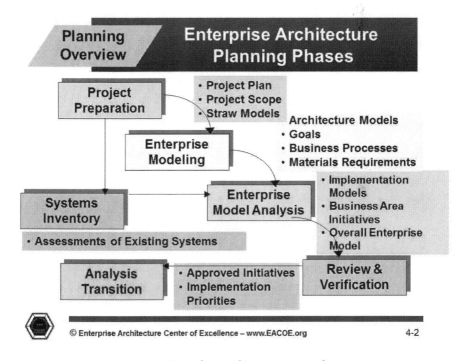

Figure 2.3 – Six Phases of Enterprise Architecture

Phase 1: Project Preparation

Project preparation includes the formation of the architecture work group, project management activities, and the creation of models and representations of the area of analysis by the Enterprise Architecture team.

The Architecture work group includes the Planning Team, Core Business Team, and Executive Review Team. Each team has a different purpose, and all three teams are required for a successful project.

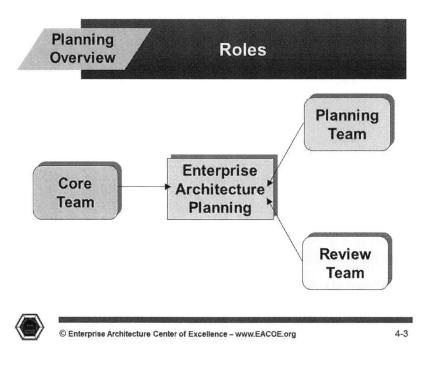

4-3

Figure 2.4 – Team Roles

The Planning Team is responsible for project deliverables, project planning, and project management. The Core Business Team is the voice of the business. It is responsible for project deliverables, communication, and acceptance. The Executive Review Team is responsible for setting the project direction, communication, and acceptance; reviewing and approving deliverables; prioritizing projects; and resolving issues that cannot be addressed by either the Planning Team or Core Business Team.

Since most people find it easier to provide feedback than to innovate, the Pinnacle Methodology uses "starter models" to launch the Enterprise Architecture Modeling phase. They may be the most time-consuming deliverables the Planning Team develops, but they are very important because they allow the Team to learn about the business. The models also demonstrate that the Team members are willing and able to roll up their sleeves and contribute. These initial efforts dramatically improve the effectiveness of the Enterprise Architecture effort and transfer the initial efforts from the business participants to the Enterprise Architecture team members. The Methodology avoids the mind-numbing, time-consuming, and intrusive interview sessions that tend to result in "top-of-mind" understandings rather than in vetted, truly long-term strategies.

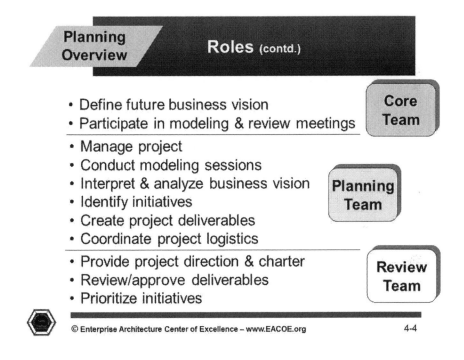

Figure 2.5 – Role Responsibilities

Phase 2: Enterprise Modeling

The purpose of the enterprise modeling phase is to describe the current understanding of the organization and its future business vision. The enterprise modeling phase begins with the architecture orientation meeting, held to formally introduce the project, set expectations, answer questions, and plan for the enterprise modeling workshops. The objective of the enterprise modeling workshop is to gain organization-wide consensus on the models and representations that describe the future business vision, current business, and target architecture. The initial "starter" models developed during the project preparation phase are used as a starting point for these workshops. Very interactive meetings and engaged participants are the norm.

Baseline Architecture Models describe the Goals, Processes, Materials, Roles, Locations, and Events that comprise the enterprise. Models are also developed that describe both the future business vision and the current state understanding. Changes will be evaluated by executive management in conjunction with the implementation of the projects defined by the Enterprise Architecture planning project initiatives.

Phase 3: Systems Inventory

The objective of the systems inventory phase is to develop an understanding of the degree and quality of automation in the organization as it exists and as it is currently planned. This phase focuses on assessing the systems used to (or being developed or acquired to) run the business. The most important aspect of this phase is documenting the business's perspective on the systems it uses to do its job. For example, the technology department may have installed very expensive systems that no longer meet the needs of the business. Such a situation will not be identified if only technology personnel are interviewed. Technology personnel should do a technical assessment, while business personnel should do a functional assessment against business needs. If there are adequate resources, the systems inventory phase can be started before the end of the enterprise modeling phase, as most organizations have limited documentation of their inventory of application or system assets.

Phase 4: Enterprise Model Analysis

The objective of the enterprise model analysis phase is to identify the set of projects required to transform the organization from its present state to its desired state. At the beginning of this phase, the Planning Team uses the Enterprise Architecture Models and systems inventory to develop Implementation Models. The Implementation Models are used to identify relationships between architectural artifacts (for example, what Processes are required to meet organizational Goals) and to refine the desired-state architecture. The Pinnacle Methodology applies statistical methods to aid the EA teams to identify and scope projects. Next, the Core Business Team and the Planning Team use their expert knowledge to assess and refine the projects, identify dependencies, and define the value proposition for each project. The projects are then prioritized based on criteria established by the Executive Review Team.

The Planning Team generally will not have enough time to thoroughly analyze all relationships in the enterprise. So, they will need to decide which of the six artifacts (Goals, Process, Materials, Roles, Locations, or Events) will initially anchor the analysis of move-ahead projects within their developed initiatives. Each of the other artifacts will be compared to the anchor artifact. Since executive management is accustomed to seeing projects based on Process, it is usually chosen as the anchor artifact. (The concepts, examples, and formulas can be translated to another anchor artifact if required.)

As with any choice of one from many, you must be aware of limits the choice inherently carries, and thus here are a few notes of consideration, a caution to keep options open and to remind you that this Methodology is best when kept flexible:

- If the analysis is anchored on a single architecture artifact or planning object, significant relationships may be overlooked. For example, a Process focus may cause associations between Materials/Data and systems to be overlooked. Material/Data associations are usually used to justify and scope master data management projects. Master Data Management is the organization, business process, system, and technical integration architecture used to create and maintain accurate and consistent views of core business data such as Customers, Products, Employees, Suppliers, and Assets. There are other priorities and easier wins.

- By selecting a Process focus, architects may also miss associations between systems and Roles and Organizations. For example, although the analysis will identify when multiple systems support that same Process—an opportunity of application portfolio rationalization that could result in cost savings through consolidating systems—additional analysis will be required to determine which organizations have automated the Process, whether any of the systems are capable of supporting the entire organization, and what the return is on consolidating the systems. The analysis needs to be done before proposing such a consolidation to executive management because its cost savings may not be worth the opportunity costs associated with the other projects.

As you can see, once the initial desired-state and as-is states models are developed, numerous analyses can be performed to provide benefits to multiple stakeholders. Extensive value is available from a Process-anchored assessment, but plan to augment it with additional assessments of high-value targeted relationships based on other business anchors—Goals, Materials, Roles, Locations, or Events—because they may help to reveal considerable opportunity.

Phase 5: Review and Verification

The first objective of the review and verification phase is to build consensus on the target architecture and the resulting projects identified to move the organization from its present state to its desired state. The second objective is to evaluate the identified projects in light of available funding, and to fund select priority projects that will have the most significant impact on the organization.

After reviewing the results of the enterprise model analysis phase, the Executive Sponsor may need to work closely with the Executive Review Team and executive management before deciding which projects to fund. During this time, the Planning Team and Core Business Team should be available to answer questions, review options, and conduct further analysis. The project prioritization meeting is held at the end of this phase to finalize the funding decisions. A member of the Executive Review Team will be selected to sponsor each of the funded projects.

Phase 6: Analysis Transition

The objective of the analysis transition phase is to ensure that the approved projects are used to implement the target architecture and result in meeting enterprise business Goals. This phase starts with educating people and communicating to them an overview of the planning process, a synopsis of the target architecture, and information about the resulting funded projects. Management then selects implementation teams for each project and assigns representatives from the Architecture Work Group to each of these implementation teams. The representatives facilitate a smooth transition from planning to implementation of architecture by working with the implementation teams on detailed scoping, analysis, and modeling.

Key components of this phase are transferring knowledge, identifying the scope of each implementation project, providing a starting point for conducting further analysis, and supporting integration and alignment. The target architecture implementation will be governed by corporate governance structures, and checkpoints will be built into the project life cycle.

Best Practices

Meeting Facilitation

Effective meeting facilitation is critical to the success of an Enterprise Architecture planning project. External facilitators or Enterprise Architecture experts can be very helpful, especially where internal politics may be sensitive, and all members of the Planning Team need to be trained in Enterprise Architecture practices. This education will give the Planning Team a set of tools that will help them streamline the project and facilitate acceptance.

A member of the Planning Team should be assigned to facilitate each meeting that only involves the Planning Team. These include starter modeling sessions, system inventory sessions, and some of the model analysis sessions. Without a facilitator, it is easy for team members to start debating details that keep them from meeting their objectives, a syndrome that is not specific to Enterprise Architecture. Alternating responsibility for meeting facilitation will improve team dynamics. The assigned facilitator should focus on meeting facilitation and not on participation, enabling the team to complete the meeting objectives. It will be a challenging, valuable experience for each facilitator. Facilitators will have an opportunity to provide content in other meetings.

An external facilitator can be used for meetings that involve the Planning Team and the Core Business Team. Such meetings include the enterprise modeling workshop and some of the meetings in the model analysis phase. Organizational dynamics generally dictate when internal or external expertise is practiced. It may be difficult for an internal staff member to objectively facilitate these key meetings, since the decisions will impact their coworkers, business partners, and internal customers. An external facilitator can insulate the Planning Team from some of the politics and enable the entire team to participate. The facilitator will need to be an expert in Enterprise Architecture concepts, terminology, requirements, deliverables, and processes. Since sensitive information will be discussed, the facilitator should, of course, sign a nondisclosure agreement (which most organizations have). What is said in these meetings should stay in these meetings, even though it rarely does. Decisions about resources to be used are very organization-specific.

Prior to key meetings, the Planning Team and facilitator should use the stakeholder analysis to identify issues to mitigate with pre-meeting communications and even to determine seating arrangements. A good facilitator will review the agenda, desired outcomes, processes, and meeting guidelines for each meeting at the beginning. He or she will also establish a shared responsibility for success.

The facilitator is responsible for keeping people focused and participating, minimizing interruptions, making sure key issues are discussed, and making sure key decisions are acknowledged and recorded. When concerns are being raised, the facilitator should recognize the point and recommend a way to address the concern. It is easy for a passionate person with a strong personality to take over a meeting. It is also common for some members of the team to question the priority of the project. If this happens, the facilitator will need to get the meeting back on track. Experienced facilitators have a tool kit that includes humor, asking "What is going on?" and enforcing process agreements. Effective facilitation is critical to the planning process.

The Planning Team will need to determine if an external facilitator is required for sessions that involve the Executive Review Team. These meetings include the architecture orientation meeting, enterprise model review sessions, and the project prioritization meeting. These meetings give the Planning Team and the Core Team an opportunity to shine.

Enterprise Architecture Tools

Over the past decades, the technology industry has started to recognize the need for Enterprise Architecture. The innovators of computer-aided systems engineering (CASE) attempted to apply and automate the rigor used in the engineering community to technology projects. Unfortunately, timing is everything, as the saying goes, and these tools were sold before most people realized how important modular design, reusability, and blueprints are. They were also designed without a clear understanding of the four pillars of Enterprise Architecture: Frameworks, Methodologies, Architecture Models, and Implementation Models.

As a result of Enterprise Architecture's increasing momentum, some vendors have created new Enterprise Architecture tools, and other vendors have modified existing tools to address needs. Some of these tools can add value by providing a semi-structured repository. Conversely, they can be a distraction, since any tool has a built-in bias of some kind—an underlying method that has been implemented in computer code, for instance—and they can introduce additional costs. In a large organization, projects routinely can be delayed by over a year if the team starts focusing on tools instead of on designing a consistent architecture for the enterprise. Selecting an Enterprise Architecture tool can create a win for the Architecture Work Group. However, selecting a tool prematurely will compromise the project when the team tries to create an architecture that fits the tool rather than do what is right for the enterprise. The combined cost of the required servers, licenses, installation, and training for some vendors' tools can easily exceed a million dollars. This may or may not be wise money spent; it all depends on the organization and its resources and must be a carefully vetted investment decision.

The Pinnacle Methodology does not recommend initially using Enterprise Architecture tools in workshops or team meetings. Sticky notes and flip charts encourage more creativity and collaboration. They are also faster and provide more flexibility. In addition, there is no setup time or learning curve, and network connections are not required. By definition, Enterprise Architecture is an approach designed to assist, not inhibit, organizations in achieving their future goals by identifying a series of business and technology improvement projects. During the Enterprise Architecture planning project, the team should focus on tasks associated with developing the strategy rather than trying to learn a new tool. Tool evaluation and purchase should be done after the first iteration of Enterprise Architecture is performed to better determine which models and artifacts are most useful to the organization. The resulting work can be used as the basis for Enterprise Architecture tool review.

Past Enterprise Architecture Efforts

Like most pioneers, organizations that have launched Enterprise Architecture efforts recognized the need for a change from the status quo and tried to build something to address it. However, most of them tried to develop an Enterprise Architecture without clear understandings of Frameworks, Methodologies, Architecture Models, or Implementation Models. While some organizations had success, most struggled with how to provide real business value quickly.

Since most organizations do not have explicit representations that describe their baseline architecture, target architecture, and roadmap, their Enterprise Architecture efforts have not been very effective. For example, while most organizations do have organizational charts and Goal names, they do not have representations that show which Processes and Materials are required to support which Goals.

During the project preparation phase, the Planning Team will review the results of the enterprise's past efforts (if any), which will be leveraged if they add value to the current Enterprise Architecture planning project. Some value is usually found in previous efforts. The Executive Sponsor and Planning Team will need to determine whether the current participation of team members from prior efforts is in the best interest of the Enterprise Architecture planning project.

Summary

The project preparation phase starts after the Enterprise Architecture planning project has been scoped, prioritized, and funded. The Enterprise Architecture methodology presented in this book has been successfully used in many organizations. While the methodology process is generally the same, the size, complexity, and culture of the organization will have a direct impact on the timeline. The first iterations of most Enterprise Architecture planning projects will take between four and seven months, although this methodology has been used to complete an Enterprise Architecture planning project in as little as forty-two days. Even there, since the team was small, the phase tasks were linear and did not show the more common overlap of multiple sub-teams that at times simultaneously pursued different arms of the project tree. The following table shows how the forty-two days were spent:

Phase	Calendar Days	EA Planning Team	Core Business Team	Executive Review Team
Project Preparation	8	8	0	0
Systems Inventory	13	13	0	0
Enterprise Modeling	9	9	5	1
Enterprise Model Analysis	10	10	0	1
Review and Verification	1	1	1	1
Analysis Transition	1	1	0	0
TOTAL	42	42	6	3

Figure 2.6 – 42-Day Enterprise Architecture Project

The remaining chapters provide more detailed process guidance, examples, suggested practices, and suggestions for success. Enterprise Architecture projects generally uncover low-hanging fruit as well as reveal more complex and exciting opportunities. Most companies prefer to keep the details of their strategies confidential, and rightly so. For this reason, the examples in the remaining chapters refer to a fictionalized company called

Sky High Gliders, whose parent company is Recreational Adventures, Inc. A single planning project is referenced in the examples to improve the consistency and flow. The appendices contain project planning checklists and additional materials from the Sky High Gliders Enterprise Architecture planning project.

CHAPTER 3

PROJECT PREPARATION

Overview

Project preparation is the first phase of the Enterprise Architecture planning project. It starts after the Executive Sponsor and Project Lead have defined the project scope and secured funding. This phase focuses on building the Architecture Work Group, establishing the project plan, developing starter models from existing materials, communicating the project phases, and securing acceptance of the project as an imperative. These steps can take anywhere from a few days to a month. The exact duration will vary based on the culture of the organization and the scope of the project. It will also vary based on the availability of the Planning Team and its experience in Enterprise Architecture. If the Planning Team is new to the Enterprise Architecture process, they should reasonably allocate additional time. At the end of this phase, all of the preparatory work required to ensure the success of the Enterprise Architecture planning project will be complete.

The Architecture Work Group

The Architecture Work Group is composed of the Planning Team, the Core Business Team, and the Executive Review Team. The size of the Planning Team will vary from five to nine people, and the size of the Core Business Team will vary from five to fifteen people. The size of the Executive Review Team will vary with the size and complexity of the organization. As long as all organizations in scope are represented, a smaller team will naturally produce higher-quality deliverables in a shorter period of time. Try to handpick members of the Planning Team and the Core Business Team. The best technologist may not be the best Enterprise Architect, just as the best carpenter may not be the best house designer. If you are not familiar with the business or organization, enlist the help of someone you trust. Make sure all members of the Executive Review Team have firsthand knowledge of the project charter and direction. The time commitment should be emphasized when recruiting Planning Team and Core Business Team members. For example, make sure they know that they need to allocate certain days to the Enterprise Modeling Workshop. Their management must be aware of this commitment.

Geographically Dispersed Teams

The Project Lead should be well versed in managing geographically dispersed teams. We have a global economy, and talented resources live all over the world. Insights from universities and corporations that have developed world-class practices for managing distributed teams have been incorporated in this book. For example, most teams need to meet in person every four to six weeks to maintain good communication and optimize productivity.

The physical location of team members can have an impact on the success of the project. Key meetings—and there are just a few that require full participation—should be conducted in person in a single location. An example key meeting from the Enterprise Architecture planning project is the Enterprise Modeling Workshop. The alternative is to hold a workshop in a central location for each geographic region. In most cases, travel will still be required; this is actually good, since people will be removed from daily routines and interactions that often consume valuable time. And this is very valuable time. Requiring physical meetings gives participants a second chance to provide input in a group setting, and it can help facilitate acceptance. That said, hosting multiple meetings in different locations can contribute to geographic stovepipes and reduce the enterprise quality of the deliverables. Multiple dispersed meetings must be managed carefully and require significant expertise. If the team uses the dispersed approach, it should extend the timeline to account for travel and for the multiple model integration rework that inevitably results.

Audio conferences and web conferences work well for meetings that do not require extensive interaction—for instance, the Enterprise Architecture orientation meeting. All relevant participants should be included in audio and web conferences if they are used; having some people dial in and others in a physical conference room creates an unequal project environment.

There will be scheduling challenges if the project team members live in different time zones, especially if they are in countries distant from each other. The team will need to get creative. It may need to create separate work groups for different regions, alternate meeting times, host duplicate meetings for different time zones, or, quite possibly, gather participants into a physical location temporarily.

A steel company with employees in the United States and Japan provided an excellent example of how to effectively manage geographically dispersed teams. Meeting schedules, language barriers, and cultural issues all posed challenges. The project was expected to take five months, but having everyone at a single location for that long would have risked a loss of personnel. The company and project team were committed to the success of the project, so they came up with a creative way to accommodate the team: they extended the timeline and people from Japan stayed in the US every other month.

For the past decade, companies have accommodated US time zones and locations. The global economy is changing, and Americans should not assume that companies will continue this practice. Language barriers and cultural issues present additional challenges. Text translators have made a lot of progress over the years, and many people speak more than one language. The best advice for working with people from different cultures is to take time to learn about their cultures, embrace diversity, and enjoy the experience. Enterprise Architecture is about explicit representations, so care is needed.

Planning Team

Being a member of the Planning Team is not for the faint of heart, and it is not for people who need to be "front and center." Planning Team members are responsible for keeping the Enterprise Architecture planning project on track. During the project preparation phase, the Planning Team focuses on building the teams, managing the project, and creating starter models. While managing the project is a priority, the team continues to contribute for the duration of the project.

In general, Planning Team members will be more effective as diplomats than as taskmasters. Planning Team members should be hardworking, analytical, organized, motivated, and able to translate words into diagrammatic representations. All Planning Team members need to have a thorough understanding of the Pinnacle Methodology. While some members of the Planning Team will know more about the business than others, they need to let members of the other teams do their jobs. Planning Team members can represent both the business and the technologists.

Core Business Team

Make sure each business unit that is in the scope of the Enterprise Architecture project has a representative on the Core Business Team. The Core Business Team needs to possess a thorough understanding of each business organization and processes. To be effective, members of the Core Business Team need to attend all modeling sessions and review meetings. Their responsibilities include sharing their business knowledge, representing that business knowledge with the assistance of the Planning Team, and defining the future vision of the organization. Core Business Team members generally come from the business and are subject matter experts in one or more of its areas.

Executive Review Team

The Executive Review Team acts as a second set of eyes. Members are typically senior staff or vice presidents that the Core Business Team reports to. The Executive Review Team is responsible for setting the project direction, communicating with other senior executives, and prioritizing projects; accepting, reviewing, and approving of the Enterprise Architecture deliverables; and resolving issues where other teams have failed to do so.

The Executive Review Team is engaged after the initial models and Enterprise Architecture artifacts are reviewed by the Core Business Team. Yes, the Executive Review Team will be able to understand these models! The Pinnacle Methodology focuses on different representations for different stakeholders, all with the requirement that they can be understood with less than five minutes of instruction. Executive Review Team members generally come from the business units, because they know the most about the business strategy and direction. When interacting with members of the Executive Review Team, keep in mind that they may have confidential information they cannot disclose. For example, they may be aware of a pending acquisition or of a facility that is closing.

Common Mistakes to Avoid

Common but avoidable mistakes include, but are not limited to: assigning one person to multiple teams, not having business leadership participation, and Planning Team members speaking on behalf of business personnel. Even if a Planning Team member has a lot of knowledge about the area under analysis, it is not appropriate to assign any one person to multiple teams. Each team—Core, Review, and Planning—has a different set of roles and responsibilities. There is a lot of work to be done, and each team needs to focus on its own responsibilities.

The purpose of most Enterprise Architecture planning projects is to plan for present and future business and technology needs and improvements. They are not successful without organization-wide agreement on, at a minimum, the Goals, Processes, and Materials requirements for the area under analysis. Real business participation is critical for verification and acceptance of the resulting architecture plan. The Planning Team should not cut short the process of developing the Enterprise Architecture by trying to speak for the business. The Planning Team is responsible for driving the project and extracting a thorough understanding of the business from the Core Business Team. To do that, the Core Business Team needs to be engaged and the Planning Team needs to practice good change management and facilitation skills.

Project Management

Project Plan

Appendix A contains checklists that identify the tasks associated with each phase of the Enterprise Architecture planning project. Use them to draft the project plan. Appendix B contains the Enterprise Architecture Quick Start Project Plan sample as well. The project should be staffed with fairly senior Enterprise Architecture personnel. Do not assume that each full-time resource has forty or more hours a week to work on project deliverables. The timeline should allow time for vacation, training, administrative tasks, and communication. Realistic, not optimistic, project planning is vital.

Project Deliverables

The Planning Team should decide where and how project deliverables are going to be stored and who has access rights. To avoid lengthy debates, one member of the Planning Team should develop a proposed approach and have the rest of the team review it. As mentioned earlier, the use of an Enterprise Architecture tool is not recommended until the first iteration of Enterprise Architecture is completed. A simple repository will do. The most common tools used to deliver Enterprise Architecture artifacts to business personnel is the extended Microsoft Office Suite, which includes Word, Excel, PowerPoint, Project, and Visio. These are not analysis tools—they are tools for delivering the resulting Enterprise Architecture to the consuming stakeholders. Some of the project outputs will contain sensitive information about the organization, projects, and stakeholders. Materials should be stored in a structure that is secure but easy to navigate, and files should have meaningful names that follow a consistent pattern. Project deliverables, working documents, meeting announcements, meeting minutes, and the issue log should be maintained in the secured repository.

Communication and Acceptance

Communication and acceptance is the responsibility of the entire Architecture Work Group. The Planning Team is responsible for developing the stakeholder analysis, stakeholder action plan, communication plan, "elevator pitch" (a concise description of the project and project benefits), and other materials required to manage communication and acceptance. The stakeholder analysis identifies which people in the organization can have the most profound impact on the Enterprise Architecture planning project. Once the key stakeholders are identified, the stakeholder analysis should include an honest assessment of how supportive each stakeholder is, key issues each stakeholder may have, what is "in it" for them, and how each stakeholder is influenced. The stakeholder analysis is used to develop the stakeholder action plan. It is also used to identify and mitigate issues with pre-meeting communications.

The communication plan is used to manage communications with the rest of the organization. It should include announcements, webcasts, "lunch and learns," and the elevator pitch. All members of the Architecture Work Group should practice the elevator pitch and use it whenever they are asked about the project.

Initial "Starter" Models

One of the most ineffective ways to launch a project is to give everyone a blank piece of paper and ask them to document their understanding of the business. Another ineffective way to launch a project is to schedule endless interviews. As a business partner, one of the most annoying things is being asked to provide information you have recently provided to several other projects. Therefore, the third set of deliverables to come out of the project preparation phase is the set of initial "starter" models.

Starter models are the most effective tool for moving an Enterprise Architecture project forward. The organization has volumes of materials that are extremely valuable and can be used to develop an initial understanding of the area under analysis. The Planning Team is responsible for collecting these materials, reviewing them, and drafting starter models. The starter models are intended to jump-start the Enterprise Architecture Modeling phase. These models provide the baseline for moving forward, begin providing traceable and verifiable analysis, and allow the leveraging of any previous efforts to dramatically accelerate the enterprise toward the end-state, architected vision. They will work with the Core Business

Team to create the target Architecture Models during the enterprise modeling phase.

Modeling Conventions

The Planning Team should not confuse people by using different modeling conventions. Rather than engaging in lengthy debates, the team should quickly define modeling conventions and move on to modeling. From a business perspective, the models are a means to an end, not an end in and of themselves. Since architects can be passionate about this topic, a brainstorming session is probably the most effective way to gain consensus on what model styles will be used. The objective of establishing conventions is to improve communication and reduce confusion. The conventions should include standards, such as level of granularity, naming conventions, and modeling notations. If needed, the conventions can be refined later in the process. Template diagrams that incorporate the conventions should be created for each type of model. Remember, there is no one model that will serve all stakeholders and abstractions in Enterprise Architecture. The objective of the business-facing Enterprise Architecture Models is business understanding.

Starter Models: Goals

Every enterprise has goals and strategies. Goals are the set of benefits or conditions that will help the enterprise achieve its objectives and implement its strategies. While they are harvesting information from the materials gathered for the project, members of the Planning Team may be asked why they are spending time building starter models when the enterprise already has a strategic plan, a mission statement, business plans, annual reports, and so on. The answer is simple: the company has many disparate documents that may or may not say the same thing. Since the enterprise probably did not have a consistent frame of reference, different deliverables were developed without regard to other deliverables that might be similar, redundant, or complementary. It is not likely that everyone will take the time to analyze a series of large, complex documents, or that they will derive the same set of goals and objectives. By analyzing the documents, reconciling any discrepancies, and developing concise visual representations, the Planning Team is much more likely to convey an accurate and consistent set of goals. The enterprise will be well served if everyone has a consistent view and understanding of the area under analysis.

The materials and information the Planning Team harvests for its initial models may include annual reports, mission statements, strategic plans, management objectives, business plans, budgets, and department plans. Once the Planning Team has collected sufficient information to understand the area under analysis, the team is ready to begin drafting models. Each model should consist of a diagram, a standard artifact name, and a template-driven definition.

Here are some tips for identifying Goals. After the tips is an illustration of the documents harvested to identify Goals and a sample starter Goal model.

- Goals describe the 'Why' column of the Enterprise Framework.

- Goals describe a benefit or condition the organization wishes to achieve in the future. An example of a benefit name is 'Reduce Costs'. An example of a name of a condition is 'Maintain Market Leadership'.

- Goals focus on desired results. An example of a desired result is 'An Increase in Promotional Activity'.

- Goals are typically measurable. An example of a measurable goal is 'Achieve repeat business by 40%'.

- Goals are typically set over a three to five year time period.

Figure 3.1 – Tips for Identifying Goals

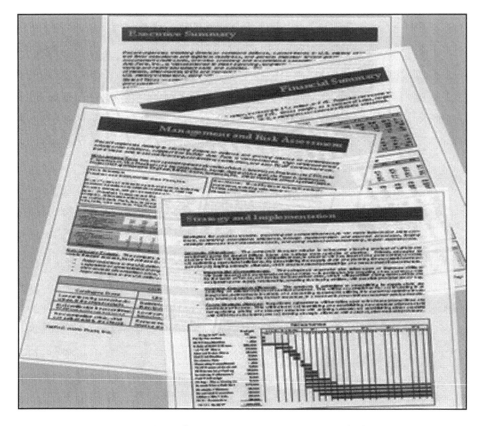

Figure 3.2 – Sample Documents Harvested to Identify Goals

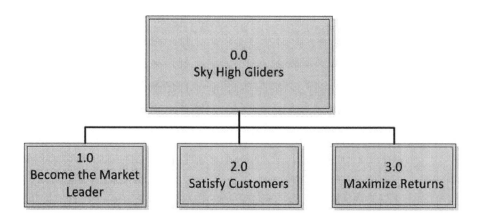

Figure 3.3 – Starter Model: Goal Names and Structure

Starter Models: Processes

After the Planning Team completes the Goal starter models, it needs to develop the Process starter models. A Process is an ongoing activity performed by the enterprise. During this phase, the Planning Team should focus on compiling the list of Processes that business units need to perform, harvesting them from the materials received. The target architecture Process models will be defined during the enterprise modeling phase. The Processes will be analyzed to determine gaps and overlaps during the modeling analysis phase.

The Planning Team will need to collect and review a myriad of documents to identify the enterprise Processes. Some of these documents include process models, business requirements, and functional specifications. Once the Processes are identified, the team should draft one or more starter models.

Here are some tips for identifying Processes and a sample Process starter model:

- Processes describe the 'How' column of the Enterprise Framework.

- Each Process is generally named with a verb and a plural noun modifier of the verb.

- Each Process can be composed of sub-processes.

- Sub-Processes further describe the parent summary process.

- Processes focus on business activities and not the organizational units that may perform the Process. Several organizational units are likely involved in any Process. An example of a business process is 'Pay Accounts'. An example of an organization is 'Accounts Payable'.

Figure 3.4 – Tips for Identifying Process

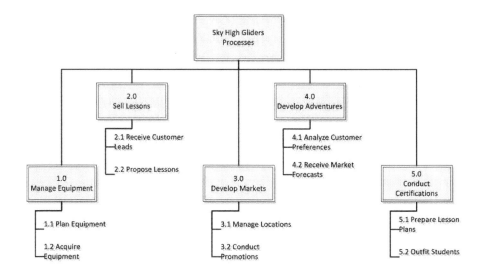

Figure 3.5 – Starter Model: Process Names and Structure

Starter Models: Materials

If an enterprise has been well designed, the data it collects should support its Goals and Processes. We use the term *Material* in the Methodology as we model data, since business materials of interest are the objects about which data is collected; that is, data represent business materials in some form. We want the Architecture Work Group to avoid falling into traps of IT-centric, data-constrained views of the area under analysis. Business users need data to answer critical questions such as "Which customers are profitable?" and "Are my products priced competitively?" If data is required to support a business Goal, a Process is required to collect, maintain, and report the data. The relationships between Enterprise Architecture artifacts are developed in the analysis phase of the Pinnacle Methodology. For example, the relationships between Materials and Goals, Processes and Goals, etc., are referred to as Implementation Models within Enterprise Architecture.

During the enterprise modeling phase, Materials provide the foundation for determining how Process and systems share data. Processes, Materials, and systems should be modeled at the same level of granularity to maintain a consistent perspective across the enterprise. *Customers* is an example of a Material. Specific attributes of a Customer, such as customer name, customer address, and customer phone number will be addressed by Implementation models.

Once the Materials are identified, the Planning team should draft a starter model diagram. Here are some tips for identifying Materials and a sample Material starter model:

> - Materials describe the 'What' column of the Enterprise Framework.
>
> - Materials are named as plural nouns.
>
> - Materials can be further modeled into other sub-Material types.
>
> - Materials support the organization, Process, and Goals, and will be shown in the Implementation Model phase of Enterprise Architecture.

Figure 3.6 – Tips for Identifying Materials

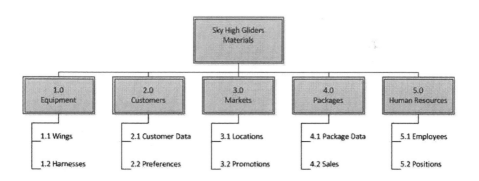

Figure 3.7 – Starter Model: Material Names and Structure

Summary

The project preparation phase starts after the Enterprise Architecture planning project is scoped, prioritized, and funded. During this phase, the Planning Team focuses on building the Architecture Work Group, project management, communication and acceptance approaches, and developing starter models. Examples of three of the six possible initial "starter" models were given. The starter models are the most critical deliverable in this phase of the Enterprise Architecture project, because they dramatically reduce the time to produce an Enterprise Architecture; they provide immediate value to the Enterprise by providing a baseline understanding of the area under analysis that is clear, unambiguous, and easy to analyze; and they are used to launch the next phase: Enterprise Modeling.

CHAPTER 4

ENTERPRISE MODELING

Overview

The purpose of the enterprise modeling phase is to achieve organization-wide consensus on the Goals, Processes, Materials, Roles, Locations, and Events that describe the enterprise area under analysis. This phase begins with an Architecture Modeling orientation meeting and proceeds to the enterprise model workshop, where the starter models created during the project preparation phase are used to launch this phase's model development. Since the best architecture will come from a consistent set of models, it is important to use the standards developed during the project preparation phase throughout the Enterprise Architecture project. It is also important to use a consistent vocabulary and to maintain the same level of granularity across the Goals, Processes, Materials, Roles, Locations, and Events models.

By the end of the workshop, the team will have a series of explicit representations that describe the enterprise area under analysis. The resulting models will be used in the enterprise model analysis phase to determine how well the current enterprise supports the mission and goals of the organization, to define and prioritize the move-ahead initiatives that will move the organization from its current state to its desired state, and to provide a baseline for other desired analyses. The models will also be used to identify how to improve the enterprise in its current state and to position it for future success.

Current and Target Architecture

Current state and target Architecture Models are both required. The current state models describe the Goals, Processes, Materials, Roles, Locations, and Events currently supporting the enterprise. The Goals are also used to determine the relative priority of projects that result from the Enterprise Architecture analysis. The target Architecture Models describe the Goals, Processes, Materials, Roles, Locations, and Events required to support the future vision of the enterprise. Roles and Location models are required when the Executive Review Team wants to consider organizational impacts during the review and verification phase.

If the target architecture is several years in the future, the Executive Review Team may want an interim set of models describing the midpoint of the plan to serve as a checkpoint. Having an interim architecture reachable in twelve to eighteen months can motivate an organization by providing a relatively quick win—or feedback about whether the organization is going "off plan." Interim architectures can also help with transition planning. The target Architecture Models will be refined during the enterprise model analysis phase.

Misconceptions about Current State and Baseline Architectures

Some architects do not believe that an understanding of the baseline architecture is required as much as is the target architecture, but most would not consider developing the target architecture without understanding key information about the industry, business, and organizations. The transition plan cannot be developed without understanding the baseline architecture. This is true in every discipline. Architects do not design and build buildings without understanding key information such as soil condition, local hazards, and regulatory requirements. Even an individual needs a starting point and an ending point for simple tasks like buying a plane ticket or going to the grocery store. Business and technology need them too. The baseline architecture is required to identify the Goals, Processes, Materials, Roles, Locations, and Events that should be created, eliminated, outsourced, or merged. How do you know that you need to create a process to support a new business unit without knowing whether it already exists? The current state, "as-is," baseline architecture should be developed after the desired-state architecture is developed.

Architecture Orientation Meeting

The architecture orientation meeting begins the enterprise modeling phase. All members of the Architecture Work Group should attend. Its objectives are to formally introduce the Enterprise Architecture project, set expectations, answer questions, and plan for the modeling workshops. But before the architecture orientation meeting, a member of the Planning Team should be assigned to meet with each member of the Core Business Team and Executive Review Team. The objectives of these preliminary meetings are to introduce the project, discuss concerns, and secure support. Having the Executive Review Team attend the architecture orientation meeting is one way it can visibly demonstrate support for its team and the Enterprise Architecture planning project.

Before hosting the architecture orientation meeting, the Planning Team should identify areas that cost the organization a lot of money, areas causing "organization pain," or areas of opportunity. If the Planning Team encounters resistance to the project and is having trouble getting buy-in, it should suggest using the most promising project as a proof of concept. For example, at one communications company, an Enterprise Architecture planning project was kicked off at the end of an internal billing crisis. The company had written off tens of millions of dollars because the systems could not account for incomplete billing records, and they needed a way to prevent similar problems. They used the Pinnacle Enterprise Architecture Methodology to target and resolve the problems and used it as a proof of concept to demonstrate Enterprise Architecture to the entire organization. A full Architecture activity was begun shortly after this success.

Enterprise Modeling Workshop

When done correctly, enterprise modeling elicits different perspectives and conflicting priorities. The job of the facilitator is to quickly drive out these perspectives, document and track mitigation of conflicts, and capture the true business of the enterprise. Enterprise modeling is about understanding each component and optimizing the whole, even at the expense of some components. This is one reason it is critical to have executive support. Remember that the objective is to optimize the *whole*, not to optimize the *part*.

Since the objective is to reach consensus on all of the enterprise models and descriptions, the facilitator must understand and drive toward it. The objective has not been met if only the Goal and Process models are created. Some models will be finalized as soon as they are reviewed. Other models need to be refined. You may even need to throw out some models and start over. The team should focus on the models that can be finalized quickly. If the team is behind schedule, it should consider a divide-and-conquer approach: time-box the activities and divide the team into subteams, each with a facilitator. The entire team should reconvene to review, integrate, and finalize the models.

Enterprise model workshops are the most effective and efficient method for executing the enterprise modeling phase and provide the most continuity and flexibility. Ideally, host the workshops on contiguous days to avoid having to refocus the team and remind it of the reasons for decisions made in previous sessions, and to avoid reopening closed issues. These issues can crop up if even a few days elapse between meetings.

Meeting Logistics and Participation

All members of the Core Business Team and Planning Team should participate in all of the modeling sessions. If a Planning Team or a Core Business Team member is no longer available, he or she should be replaced with another subject matter expert. Make sure every affected business unit and functional area is represented in the modeling sessions. The exact number of participants will vary by organization.

Face-to-face meetings are highly desirable. There is a full agenda, a lot of interaction is required, and confidential information will be discussed. These meetings are not the time to use conference calls, web meetings, or video conferences. A combination of larger conference rooms and additional smaller rooms should be reserved in case the group needs to create subteams to expedite the process. To be effective, everyone will need to stay focused on the workshop. If possible, the modeling sessions should be held off-site to avoid interruptions. If at all possible, meeting participants should turn off their laptops, cell phones, and other mobile devices during the meeting.

The agenda, objectives, starter models, and key issues must be delivered to all participants several working days before the first day of the modeling workshop. Flip charts, markers, sticky-note pads, and pens should be provided during the meeting—they work better than automated tools (really!) Easily-referenced source documents that hold key information should be brought to the meeting. Avoid participant burnout by keeping the first meeting to a reasonable length and provide regular breaks. Providing beverages, light and healthy snacks, and meals will also help keep people engaged and focused.

Sometimes the Core Business Team gets excited about a particularly high-focus topic and strays from the agenda. Many participants capture and feed off this excited energy, but the facilitator may determine that the team needs to be reined in and directed toward other topics. If there is a lot of synergy between workshop participants, they may be able to exceed the meeting objectives without sticking to a rigorous agenda. If the meeting strays too far, the Planning Team may need to rework the agenda to make sure that a complete set of enterprise models results from the workshop.

The remainder of this section assumes that models have been built independently of each other—a Goal model, a Process model, a Materials model, and so on. These are Architecture Models. Another set of models—Implementation Models—relate Enterprise Architecture artifacts to each other. An example is Goals that can only be achieved through required Processes. Some organizations prefer to schedule discussions of different functional areas on different workshop days. For this, use the process described in the following section and create the Goal, Process, and Materials models for each functional area. A small organization or project might be able to address all enterprise models in a single day, but this is rare, especially in the first attempt at Enterprise Architecture. If separate workshops are scheduled for different functional business areas, a consolidation workshop or session will be required; however, this approach may raise additional conflicts and should be avoided if possible.

Using Interviews to Supplement the Workshop

If used with some caution, personal interviews can *supplement* the Enterprise Architecture planning process. A mixture of workshops and personal interviews can suggest a sort of "class structure" among participants. Strive to use interviews only to accommodate individuals who have unique insights and who also cannot participate in the modeling workshops—for example, a senior executive who cannot risk discussing sensitive information in front of a group of people. Another example might be a key resource located in another country who cannot travel for a reason such as a family crisis or disability.

That said, personal interviews can be an effective way to gather the initial information required to create starter models and build momentum. After the project is in motion, the modeling workshops are required to update the models, gain consensus, and establish a shared responsibility for success. Interviews can also be used to develop the architecture for a specific project or a very small organization. However, they are not an alternative approach to developing the architecture for a large, complex enterprise. The impact on the quality of the deliverables, stakeholder buy-in, and project timeline is very significant. Workshops are the preferred approach in all cases, and significant effort should be expended to attempt the workshop approach to Enterprise Architecture.

When planning for interviews, do not underestimate the levels of skill or effort required to conduct individual interviews. In addition to understanding Enterprise Architecture, the interviewer will need to prepare for the interview, convince people that the project is important, draw information out of people, share insights gained in other interviews, propose alternatives, and stick to a schedule. Prior to each interview, the interviewer should anticipate questions and develop a presentation that the interviewee can relate to.

The interviewer may need to work with the rest of the Planning Team to create a consistent set of Enterprise Architecture Model diagrams containing different components and levels of granularity for different audiences. If this is done, the models should be labeled as submodels to avoid confusion. This is one reason Enterprise Architecture is considered both a science and an art: the rendering needs to suit the audience. The materials to be discussed should be sent to the interviewee a few days ahead to give him or her an opportunity to review the models before the meeting.

Some members of the Core Business Team will want to be interviewed in lieu of participating in the modeling workshop. However, you should understand that developing enterprise models via personal interviews takes a lot more time, challenges consensus, and actually produces lower-quality models. It takes a lot longer because the Planning Team needs to schedule, prepare for, and conduct a series of disparate interviews. Next, it needs to consolidate meeting notes, share information, reconcile differences, and update models. Then, it needs to present the updates to the people who were interviewed and start the cycle again. People do not buy in because they do not hear the other perspectives and have no opportunity to participate in either reaching a consensus or negotiating a compromise. Individual interviews should be reserved for rare situations in which a person is unable to participate in a workshop for reasons that cannot be mitigated.

Goal Modeling Sessions

The Planning Team will kick off the Goal modeling session by introducing the Core Business Team to the starter models developed by the Planning Team. The Core Business Team will refine the models as they deem necessary. Traceability of changes—the ability to track an assertion or decision back to an authoritative, documented source—is a must. This is not a top-of-mind approach, as are most traditional interview-based approaches. After the team reaches consensus on the final set of Goals, they will re-model them, develop a "human-consumable" diagram, and add to the template descriptions as required.

The team should understand how Goals are defined. A Goal describes a benefit or a condition the organization wishes to achieve in the future. The team should also understand that Goals are used to determine whether activities the organization performs today need to be changed to better support the future vision and Goals. Refer back to the starter model section of this book for hints on identifying Goals. Review the hints with the Core Business Team at the beginning of the Goal modeling session.

The Planning Team needs to think objectively during the modeling workshops. The Core Business Team will immediately review and approve some of the models, while other models will need to be explained, refined, or possibly discarded as interim work. All of these changes need careful traceability (as will all models and changes). If the Core Business Team understands that the models are designed to solicit feedback, they will appreciate each work effort. The Planning Team should not feel as though changes to its models mean that it wasted its time or that it is being judged. If members of the Core Business Team respond emotionally, the meeting facilitator should attempt to remove the emotion from the situation. He or she may use humor as a possible approach, or remind everyone of the process to get everyone focused on creating an accurate set of models.

In the beginning of the sessions, the team should not focus on presentation aesthetics. Goals will be written on sticky notes and placed on a wall or board. As trivial as they may sound, sticky notes are not optional; they are the *preferred* approach. The teams work the models rather than work a tool. This low-tech approach has proven to be the fastest way to review options and achieve consensus. The sticky notes enable the team to add Goals, move Goals around, group Goals, and remove Goals; this type of visualization is vital to achieve a complete understanding of the Goal models.

Since an architecture project can identify numerous Goals, it stands to reason that every goal is not independent or equally important. After the Goals are grouped and rated, they are placed in a format that is easily reviewed. The final Goal model is presented in a diagram that takes the following form:

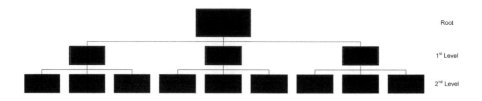

Figure 4.1 – Generic Enterprise Architecture Model Diagram

Since Goals are the first set of models discussed with the Core Business Team, the following types of questions can be posed to initiate the discussion.

- What is our business today?

- What will our business be a few years from now?

- Will there be a shift in priorities in the short term? In the long term?

- What is the most important objective for the next twelve to twenty-four months?

The kinds of Goals appearing in your list will differ depending on whether you are modeling an entire organization, a division, a department, or a project. Goals may conflict because departments, divisions, or business segments generally exist in different parts of the organization with differing Goals. For example, the Marketing department may be working toward a Goal Name such as "Increase our global exposure by investing in three more Internet marketing tools by the third quarter of next year." On the other hand, the technology department might be working toward a Goal Name such as "Decrease new systems expenditures by 7 percent by the end of the next fiscal year as measured by year-over-year costs." Once all of the Goals are defined, the team will begin to realize that optimizing the Goals for the entire organization might be to the detriment of some parts of the organization. This is where things can get emotional and shows why you need a professional facilitator and executive support.

By the end of the modeling session, the Goals should be graphically arranged into a logical representation, beginning with a root level and advancing through each sublevel of the Goal model diagram. Sometimes the starter models assembled by the Planning Team are close to complete, but sometimes they have holes. The Core Business Team is responsible for correcting any errors and filling in gaps.

Describing Goals

In addition to graphically identifying the Goals of the enterprise, it is important to provide a template-based, textual description for each Goal. These descriptions are a required output of the modeling sessions and accompany the Goal model diagram; they are actually more important than the Goal names themselves. The Goal definitions should be specific and follow a consistent, enterprise-wide template. They need to contain the name of the Goal, the desired result, the way they will be measured, and the timeframe for success.

Here is an illustration of a sample Goal name model:

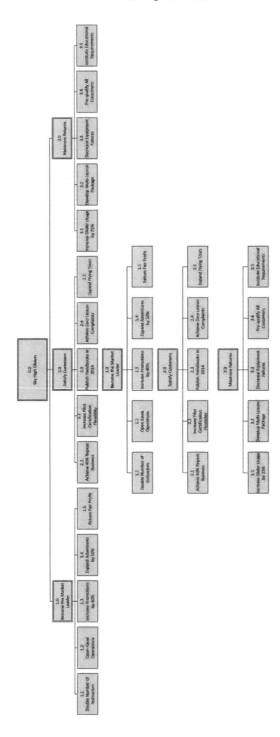

Figure 4.2 – Goal Name Model Diagram

The following table shows the descriptions for each object in the Goal model:

Goal Name	Description
0.0 Sky High Gliders' Mission	Sky High Gliders' Mission is to lead the industry in providing our customers with the most pleasurable, exciting and safe paragliding lessons and adventures in Hawaii.
1.0 Become the Market Leader	Become the Market Leader strives to rank ahead of our competitors resulting in the largest number of instructors, locations, and pilot hours booked in the region, and will be measured by obtaining 30% of the market share by 2016.
1.1 Double Number of Instructors	Double Number of Instructors strives to firmly establish Sky High Gliders as the largest paragliding operation throughout Maui, Oahu, and the Big Island of Hawaii, resulting in the ability to offer more paragliding lessons, and will be measured by hiring fifteen instructors certified by the United States Hang Gliding and Paragliding Association, Inc. (USHPA) within the next fiscal year.
1.2 Open Kauai Operations	Open Kauai Operations strives to expand our geographic coverage, resulting in the ability to meet growing customer demand and will be measured by establishing an operational base in Kauai by the end of the next fiscal year.
1.3 Increase Promotions by 40%	Increase Promotions by 40% strives to increase promotional coverage, resulting in more knowledge and insight to adventure-based travel agents and promotion of the exciting appeal of paragliding and will be measured by a 40% increase in promotions over the next three years.

	Goal Name	Description
1.4	Expand Adventures by 50%	Expand Adventures by 50% strives to increase the number of and types of adventures offered, resulting in the ability to offer more pilot training programs and tandem flights than any competitor, and will be measured by a 50% increase in adventure types over the next three years.
1.5	Return Fair Profit	Return Fair Profit strives to generate a fair profit, resulting in satisfaction of the financial objectives of Sky High's parent Recreational Adventures, Inc. and will be measured by a 25% increase in profit on continuing operations over the next three years.
2.0	Satisfy Customers	Satisfy Customers strives to ensure all aspects of the customer's expectations are met or exceeded, resulting in happy customers, and will be measured by the reception of positive customer feedback and number of repeat customers each fiscal year.
2.1	Achieve 40% Repeat Business	Achieve 40% Repeat Business strives to ensure customers return to Sky High Gliders, resulting in an increase in customer satisfaction, and will be measured by the 40% of the customer base being repeat customers each fiscal year .

Goal Name	Description
2.2 Increase Pilot Certification Flexibility	Increase Pilot Certification Flexibility strives to offer a variety of pilot certification packages, class times, and free memberships to the local flying club, resulting in a higher customer satisfaction and will be measured by an increase in types of certification packages offered, an additional class time offered daily, and the development of a partnership with the local flying club by the end of the fiscal year
2.3 Publish Handbooks	Publish Handbooks strives to publish handbooks detailing detail how to get started, basic flying techniques, equipment needed, tips for new pilots, how to conduct weather briefings, and places to paraglide around the world, resulting in satisfied customers, and potential new business and will be measured by the release of 3 handbooks in the next two years.
2.4 Achieve Zero Lesson Complaints	Achieve Zero Lesson Complaints strives to never receive a customer complaint, regarding the instruction received, resulting in satisfied customers, and will be measured by regularly reviewing our pilots and responding to customer feedback provided in surveys each month.
2.5 Expand Flying Tours	Expand Flying Tours strives to offer greater choices in types, duration, and launch locations on each island, resulting in greater flexibility and ability for personalized options, and will be measured by the purchase of new equipment each fiscal year.

Goal Name	Description
3.0 Maximize Returns	Maximize Returns strives to provide the greatest possible fair monetary return to our corporate owner, resulting in continual profit and growth opportunities, and will measured by maximizing utilization by 25% and minimizing losses by 15% in the next two years
3.1 Increase Glider Usage by 25%	Increase Glider Usage by 25% strives to expand the daily usage of our fleet, resulting in more revenue and expansion, and will be measured by an average of 25% over the next two fiscal years.
3.2 Develop Multi-Lesson Package	Develop Multi-Lesson Package strives to offer lesson packages, resulting in the improvement of long term instructor and glider scheduling visibility, and will be measured by the announcement and publication of the package details within the next fiscal year.
3.3 Decrease Equipment Failures	Decrease Equipment Failures strives to reduce the rate of equipment failures resulting in the highest quality gear available and regular inspections and maintenance, and will be measured by a reduction in the failure rate by 20% over the next three fiscal years.
3.4 Pre-qualify All Customers	Pre-qualify All Customers strives to strictly pre-qualify all prospective previously rated pilots, resulting in a decreased risk of equipment loss or damage, and will be measured by the reception of completed qualification papers from every rated pilot each time a charter is booked.

Goal Name	Description
3.5 Institute Education Requirements	Institute Education Requirements strives to offer a fun and educational paragliding overview for first time customers, resulting in the reduction of risk of accidents, and will be measured by the creation, training, and adoption of educational requirements by the end of the fiscal year.

Figure 4.3 – Goal Names and Descriptions

After the Goals are identified, they should be reviewed by the Planning Team to determine which are tactical and which are strategic. Generally, strategic Goals will have a more significant impact on the target architecture than tactical Goals. Tactical Goals will be used to determine the relative priority and sequence of projects in the short term. Years ago, Goals were considered strategic if they would take five to seven years to accomplish. Today, Goals that can be accomplished in less than two years are generally considered tactical Goals, and Goals that take more than that are considered strategic. However, since the fast pace of business change has been amplified, especially with every new social media and smartphone advancement, each organization will have its own unique interpretation of the strategic-versus-tactical demarcation.

Review and Approval

If at all possible, the Goal models and descriptions should be reviewed by the Executive Review Team and prioritized before proceeding to the other models that make up the Enterprise Architecture. This operation can be done in the last hour of the workshop's review day. Such participation in the modeling sessions, which provides relevant feedback to the work of the Planning and Core teams' models, provides an effective and positive way for executives to visibly demonstrate commitment and support for the project.

Process Modeling Sessions

The approach for modeling Processes is similar to the approach for modeling Goals. The agenda, objectives, expectations, and approach that will be the basis of process modeling should be discussed at the beginning of each modeling session. The facilitator should also establish a shared responsibility for success among all teams involved in the modeling sessions.

The Process starter models are reviewed at the beginning of the Process modeling session and are not expected to be perfect. Remember, they were designed to kick off the modeling workshop and solicit feedback from the subject matter experts. In all probability, the Core Business Team will need to add and/or delete Processes and update models during the workshop. Hints for identifying Processes were included in this book's discussion of the starter model session. These hints should be reviewed with the Core Business Team at the beginning of the Process modeling session.

Differentiating Process and Organizations

Something that should be addressed early in the workshop is the fact that people want to see themselves and their roles in the Process models. People may be looking for an indication that the Processes they perform are going to be outsourced or moved to another group, so it can be a sensitive issue. Some members of the team, especially long-term employees who have survived several rounds of layoffs, may feel like they might be adversely impacting the lives and livelihoods of coworkers who are friends. Formal and informal communications need to be appropriately managed, because these people are not always easy to read and understand. The Project Lead needs to keep the team focused on the objectives and to be prepared to swiftly replace people not up to the task at hand. Modeling Processes are not about modeling the people who perform the Processes; this is an Implementation Model. *Process is performed by role* is an example of an Implementation Model (we will discuss them in a later chapter).

The Planning Team can proactively address this area of sensitivity by explaining the difference between a Process and a Role. Processes and Roles are modeled separately when building Architecture Models in Enterprise Architecture. Processes deal with business activities, not organizational units or roles that perform them. For example, "Accounts Payable" is an organization, while "Pay Accounts" is a Process Name. Each organization usually performs several Processes, and a single Process is often performed by multiple organizations and roles. It is counterproductive to create separate Processes for multiple organizations if they are performing the same Process. The following illustration shows how multiple organizations execute the same "Monitor Budget Performance" Process.

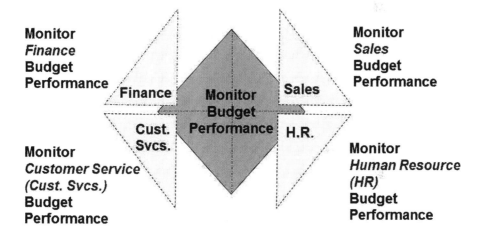

Figure 4.4 – Process to Role/Organization Model

Binding Process to Other Enterprise Architecture Artifact Models

Having a relatively high number of Processes can keep an organization from generalizing Processes or associating them with Materials, Roles and Organizations, Locations, and Events too quickly—the situation in most organizations today. Binding Processes to Organizations too quickly can keep people from identifying consolidation opportunities. For example, it might make sense to consolidate logistics systems, but if one system is bound to the manufacturing organization and another is bound to the support organization, the opportunity will not be identified. To realize opportunities to reduce costs by eliminating redundancies, we must see that Processes are redundant first.

Several years ago, a company in the high-tech sector wanted to reduce its number of Processes. They proposed using the manufacturing business Processes and systems to run the professional services organization. The rationale for this proposal was that "people are similar to products," "skills are similar to parts," and "consulting projects are similar to custom-built products." The organization countered, raising the argument that force-fitting professional services' Processes, systems, and data into a manufacturing model could compromise the organization. How were emotions removed from the equation? They modeled each business area, compared and contrasted them, and drew the conclusion based on these business-approved models, that yes, significant synergies *did* exist. It was not *that* radical, after all.

Differentiating Process from Business Process Improvements

Having attainable Goals is critical to the success of any organization. The Process models tell us what has to be done in an organization. The Processes-to-Goals Implementation Model will show which Processes are required to achieve particular Goals, which may cause the Core Business Team to immediately start thinking about business process improvements—opportunities that naturally occur when explicit and clear representations are developed and analyzed. Enterprise Architecture is *not* about technology per se but about *helping the business run better.* While discussions about improving business processes are very important, the team needs to stay focused on the task at hand. It is already a challenge to have members of the Core Business Team dedicate time to something as intense as this workshop, so such distracting and off-topic discussions only reduce the Core Team's workshop effectiveness. If the objectives of the workshop are not met, additional days will need to be added to the modeling workshop. Focus is required. A lot of opportunities result from these modeling efforts, so they need to be given the attention they deserve.

People often confuse Process with business process flow. Unlike Business Processes, there is no reference to process flow or organization in Processes. A Process represents the steps to get something done within the enterprise. Process flows are described by sequences of Processes or by a Process-to-data relationship diagram. Some members of the Core Business Team would rather look at process improvements than develop models that describe the enterprise, but this can be a next step once the Enterprise Architecture is completed. Let the Core Business Team know that business process improvements can be addressed by the implementation projects funded at the end of the Enterprise Architecture planning project. If they stick to the methodology, they will see how Process supports Goals.

Creating the Process Model

Processes can be related to subprocesses, and subprocesses may need to be further understood through sub-subprocesses. The sticky note method used to create Goal models will be used to create the Process model. This method makes it very easy for the team to quickly create and review what-if scenarios by adding, deleting, moving, and grouping Processes; the team will not take long to eliminate redundant Processes and non-value-added activities. After the Processes are identified, the team should represent the full Process model.

Textual descriptions need to be created for each Process and subprocess. To ensure key information is represented in the descriptions, the Planning Team should create templates for the definitions of Processes. The following illustration shows the descriptions for the Sky High Gliders processes and subprocesses using standardized templates for Processes and subprocess descriptions.

Here is an illustration of a sample Process name model:

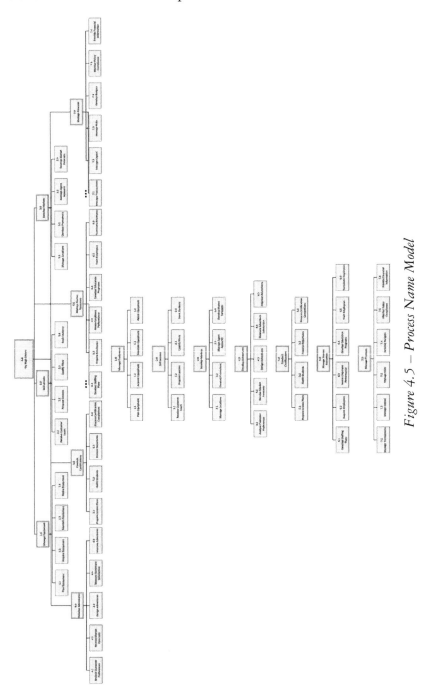

Figure 4.5 – Process Name Model

	Process Name	Description
0.0	Sky High Gliders Processes	Sky High Gliders Processes is concerned with performing the activities required to achieve its mission, goals and objectives.
1.0	Manage Equipment	Manage Equipment is concerned with overseeing all equipment including planning, acquiring, maintaining and disposing tangible goods directly involved with delivering our service to customers.
1.1	Plan Equipment Needs	Plan Equipment Needs involves forecasting and recommending changes to the quantity and type of equipment owned by Sky High Gliders.
1.2	Acquire Equipment	Acquire Equipment involves identifying equipment acquisition needs, ordering equipment from qualified suppliers and accepting equipment in fulfillment of those orders.
1.3	Maintain Equipment	Maintain Equipment involves keeping equipment in peak operating condition.
1.4	Retire Equipment	Retire Equipment involves disposing of equipment no longer needed in the most cost-effective manner.
2.0	Sell Lessons	Sell Lessons is concerned with completing sales of lessons including identifying and satisfying the requirements of prospective students, qualifying those prospective students and accepting lesson requests.

	Process Name	Description
2.1	Receive Customer Leads	Receive Customer Leads involves identifying prospective customers and their lesson desires.
2.2	Propose Lessons	Propose Lessons involves providing lesson packages matching the needs of prospective customers.
2.3	Qualify Pilots	Qualify Pilots involves validating the skills of prospective previously rated pilots.
2.4	Book Students	Book Students involves confirming a customer's lesson package purchase and schedule required equipment and personnel.
3.0	Develop Markets	Develop Markets is concerned with creating expansion in the number of prospective customers including managing locations, conducting promotions, managing agent account, and developing market forecasts.
3.1	Manage Locations	Manage Locations involves planning, acquiring, and maintaining base locations.
3.2	Conduct Promotions	Conduct Promotions involves enhancing and expanding the market's knowledge of and desire for Sky High Gliders.
3.3	Manage Agent Accounts	Manage Agent Accounts involves enhancing the effectiveness of travel agents as a distribution channel for our adventures.
3.4	Develop Market Forecasts	Develop Market Forecasts involves assessing future market needs and conditions.

	Process Name	Description
4.0	Develop Adventures	Develop Adventures is concerned with growing the types of adventures offered including defining and releasing new adventure offerings and enhancing current adventure offerings.
4.1	Analyze Customer Preferences	Analyze Customer Preferences involves assessing customer preference information.
4.2	Receive Market Forecasts	Receive Market Forecasts involves collecting market forecast information.
4.3	Design Adventures	Design Adventures involves creating the definition and structure of new offerings, such as where the adventure is located, what adventure options are available, if any promotions will be required for the new adventure and the pricing of each adventure.
4.4	Measure Adventure Satisfaction	Measure Adventure Satisfaction involves analyzing customer evaluations determining their relative satisfaction over time.
4.5	Improve Adventures	Improve Adventures involves gathering and analyzing the information required to enhance glider adventure definitions based on customer evaluations.
5.0	Conduct Certifications	Conduct Certifications is concerned with performing our pilot certification program including preparing lesson plans, outfitting students and processing departures and certifications.

	Process Name	Description
5.1	Prepare Lesson Plans	Prepare Lesson Plans involves ensuring the lesson plans for all students choosing to receive pilot certification are created and approved by the Senior Instructor.
5.2	Outfit Students	Outfit Students involves gathering all equipment ensuring gear fits properly before certification begins.
5.3	Process Departures	Process Departures involves orienting the customers to the particular glider configuration and optional equipment included in the glider package, briefing customers on local weather patterns and handing out guidebooks and aviation charts.
5.4	Process Certification Completions	Process Certification Completions involves processing proficiency and certification paperwork, inspecting and cleaning equipment and seeking customer feedback on certification process.
6.0	Manage Human Resources	Manage Human Resources is concerned with overseeing Human Resource needs including planning, acquiring, supervising, developing and terminating the employees.
6.1	Develop Staffing Plans	Develop Staffing Plans involves assessing future requirements for employees based on manpower and skilling requirements of the enterprise.
6.2	Acquire Employees	Acquire Employees involves recruiting, offering and accepting new employees.

	Process Name	Description
6.3	Assess Employee Performance	Assess Employee Performance involves assigning, controlling and assessing performance of work performed by employees.
6.4	Develop Education Programs	Develop Education Programs involves enhancing and expanding employee skills, including but not limited to, preparation for the new glider services. It is anticipated that these programs will become the foundation for the education glider services which will be offered in the future.
6.5	Train Employees	Train Employees involves identifying the training needs of individual employees, enrolling employees into specific classes and conducting the training classes.
6.6	Terminate Employees	Terminate Employees involves removing the relationship between the enterprise and employee.
7.0	Manage Finances	Manage Finances is concerned with acquiring, controlling and reporting the fiscal requirements including managing transactions, capital, and risks, developing budgets, monitoring policy compliance, and providing financial information.
7.1	Manage Transactions	Manage Transactions involves identifying, classifying and controlling monetary transactions in accordance with generally accepted accounting principles.
7.2	Manage Capital	Manage Capital involves acquiring and safeguarding the financial resources.

	Process Name	Description
7.3	Manage Risks	Manage Risks involves controlling the variability of financial returns due to the risks inherent in our industry.
7.4	Develop Budgets	Develop Budgets involves receiving budget constraints from the parent organization, allocating and controlling funding of individual organization units through time and obtaining approval of Sky High Gliders' budget priorities from RAI.
7.5	Monitor Policy Compliance	Monitor Policy Compliance involves auditing conformance to the stated policies of the enterprise and making recommendations for changes to either the operational practices or corporate policies where appropriate.
7.6	Provide Financial Information	Provide Financial Information involves collecting, analyzing, formatting and publishing financial results to internal and external organizations.

Figure 4.6 – Process Descriptions

Process Modeling Techniques

The two Process modeling techniques that can be used to develop and stimulate the Process models activities are the Resource Life Cycle technique and the Input/Process/Output Process technique. The Resource Life Cycle Model technique suggests that for each first-level Process, there could be set of associated planning, acquiring, utilization, disposal, and monitoring Processes that can be discovered. The technique provides a good way to test for completeness by testing each Process verb to see which ones make sense for each Process. The Input/Process/Output discovery technique suggests that most Processes require one or more input Processes, a Process for transformation, and Process to produce one or more outputs.

The following tables outline how each technique could be used to identify Processes:

Process Name		1.0 Collect Overdue Receivables
Sub-Process		
Plan	<Resource>	1.1 Plan collection activities
Acquire	<Resource>	1.2 Acquire list of overdue receivables
Use	<Resource>	1.3 Use accounting process for receivables
Dispose	<Resource>	1.4 Close receivables account
Monitor	<Resource>	1.5 Monitor overdue receivables progress

Figure 4.7 – Resource Life Cycle Technique

Process Name		1.0 Pay Bills
Sub-Process		
Input	<noun>	1.1 Gather *due bills*
Process	<noun>	1.2 Process *payments*
Output	<noun>	1.3 Mail *checks*

Figure 4.8 – Input/Process/Output Technique

Review and Approval

After the Process models and descriptions are created, the Executive Review Team should review and approve them. Participating in the modeling sessions enables the executives to provide feedback early enough in the methodology to minimize rework.

Materials Modeling Sessions

The Business Materials are those objects about which the business collects data. Materials modeling methodology is similar to the methodology used to model Goals and Processes. The Planning Team should have distributed the Materials starter models, and the participants should have reviewed the models before the workshop. Hints for identifying Materials were included in the starter model section of this book. These hints should be reviewed with the Core Business Team at the beginning of the Materials modeling session.

Before introducing the starter models, the facilitator should remind everyone that Materials are a critical component of the enterprise model analysis phase. The level of detail used to model Materials should be consistent with the level of detail used to model Processes and Goals. (This session is not the forum to discuss detailed attributes such as customer name or implementation details.) When complete, the enterprise models should have a consistent level of granularity across all architecture components.

There should also be a consistent perspective across all areas of the business. Some participants will want to place too much emphasis on the area of the business they know best, because they feel their jobs are at risk or because they believe it is all they know. Regardless of the reason for these biases, the facilitator is responsible for reminding everyone to keep a balanced focus and encourage their active participation and contributions. Remind reticent participants that the assessment also reveals many new and challenging opportunities that someone will need to address, and that these opportunities often offset any attrition of skills and business areas found to be less effective with respect to the future target architecture. Participants are thus in the driver's seat to identify emerging opportunities that will have lasting value to the enterprise. If *this* realization doesn't encourage them, perhaps they are not viable participants.

When modeling, it is important to separate abstraction from instantiation. For example, the job, work product, skills, and the person doing the job are modeled separately. This way, the person doing the job today can do a different job tomorrow, a job can be automated, or the skills associated with the job can change.

The first step in modeling Materials is to use sticky notes, as with other models, to identify missing Materials. Then the sticky notes are grouped and duplicates are merged. Once the Materials models are finalized, descriptions are created for each Material.

Here is an example of a Material name model. The Materials descriptions are shown below the Materials name model.

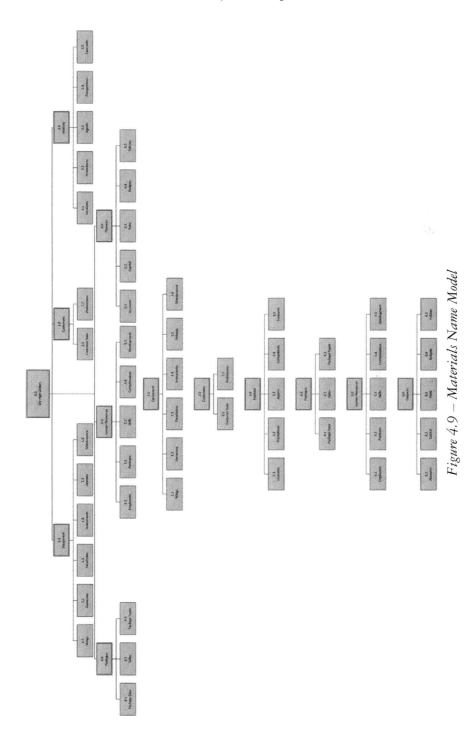

Figure 4.9 – Materials Name Model

	Material Name	Description
0.0	Sky High Gliders Materials	The high level categories of Materials necessary to support Sky High Gliders.
1.0	Equipment	Equipment classifies and describes the physical assets obtained and maintained by Sky High Gliders.
1.1	Wings	Wings represent the structure used to allow the glider to fly.
1.2	Harnesses	Harnesses represent the pilots "sling" and attachments holding them in the gliders' wings.
1.3	Parachutes	Parachutes represent the emergency system that is used in case of a glider problem.
1.4	Instruments	Instruments represent instruments used during flight such as vario-altimeters and Push-to-talk (PTT) radios.
1.5	Helmets	Helmets represent head coverings worn during flight to prevent head injuries.
1.6	Maintenance	Maintenance represents the nature and quality of the equipment needed for lessons and adventures.
2.0	Customers	Customers classify and describe the types, qualifications and preference of those individuals who have purchased or wish to purchase lessons and adventure packages.
2.1	Customer Data	Customer Data customers and describing their characteristics, packages reserved and packages completed.

	Material Name	Description
2.2	Preferences	Preferences represent the stated and / or historical packages, location, and adventure option preference of customers.
3.0	Markets	Markets classify and describe the geographic areas we serve, the market segments from which our customer come, and our activities which promote and estimate Sales.
3.1	Locations	Locations represent the geographic areas we serve.
3.2	Promotions	Promotions represent the plans, targets, and media used to promote lessons and adventures
3.3	Agents	Agents represent the individual associates with an agency that interact with customers on behalf of Sky High Gliders.
3.4	Competitors	Competitors represent the organizations that offer alternative or competing recreational services to our customer base.
3.5	Forecasts	Forecasts represent estimates of future market conditions and Sales.
4.0	Packages	Packages classify and describe our package offerings to customers.

	Material Name	Description
4.2	Sales	*Sales* represents customers' agreements to purchase lesson and adventure packages from Sky High Gliders.
4.3	Package Types	*Package Types* represents, classifies, and distinguishes our package offerings.
5.0	Human Resources	*Human Resources* classifies and describes the employees and contractors who perform work for the enterprise and their relationships with it.
5.1	Employees	*Employees* represents identifications of the human resources who perform work for the enterprise.
5.2	Positions	*Positions* represents the job descriptions and departmental authorizations for personnel.
5.3	Skills	*Skills* represent human resource capabilities derived from educational or on-the-job experiences.
5.4	Compensation	*Compensation* represents the monetary and nonmonetary entitlements given to human resources in exchange for work.
5.5	Development	*Development* represents the opportunities to enhance and expand the capabilities of human resources.
6.0	Finances	*Finances* classifies and describe the tangible and intangible property used to support the operations of the enterprise.
6.1	Accounts	*Accounts* represent the fiscal transactions of the enterprise.

	Material Name	Description
6.0	Finances	Finances classify and describe the tangible and intangible property used to support the operations of the enterprise.
6.1	Accounts	Accounts represent the fiscal transactions of the enterprise
6.2	Capital	Capital represents the financial instruments used to supply the enterprise with financial resources.
6.3	Risks	Risks represent potential losses to the enterprise's financial position and measures taken to minimize such losses.
6.4	Budgets	Budgets represent the allocation of financial resources to Sky High Gliders organization units through time.
6.5	Policies	Policies represent the financial rules, policies and guidelines which must be followed in order to accurately represent the financial condition of the business.

Figure 4.10 – Materials Descriptions

Review and Approval

After the team creates the Materials models and descriptions, the deliverables should be reviewed and approved by the Executive Review Team at the end of the Material modeling session rather than wait until all models are complete.

Modeling Roles, Locations, and Events

The Roles, Locations, and Events models are summarized below. The same methods, techniques, and approaches to model these Enterprise Architecture artifacts are used as those followed for Goals, Processes, and Materials.

Roles perform Processes on behalf of the enterprise. The Roles model should reflect both the skills needed in the future desired state and the current state skills within the organization. If the architecture effort is targeted at a specific project, the department manager, program manager, or project manager should be able to provide input to this model. Note that this is not an organization chart or a list of job names—hence the use of the term *skills*.

The initial depth of the Roles model depends on the project scope. The internal Roles model for a public company would contain business units, divisions, and departmental roles. Third-party organizations, such as key vendors, suppliers and outsourcing partners, should be included in the Roles model since some responsibility is being handed to these vendors. To understand the importance of including partners, consider the example of payroll processing: even though the actual payroll process might be handled by a third-party vendor, the client company is responsible for its delivery to its stakeholders. The Internal Revenue Service is not going to accept outsourcing as an excuse for not paying taxes.

Locations are the sites where work is performed. Most internal Locations will be corporate offices and facilities types. Security, Human Resources, Facilities, or Legal functional areas could also have a list of internal locations. Contracts, sourcing, or vendor relations functional areas could have a list of external organizations. Of course, the best source for developing the initial models is always to harvest from existing materials as usual. If a list of locations is not generated from these sources, each member of the Core Business Team and Planning Team could aid the workshop by providing a list ahead of time.

Events are all of the types of stimulus the Enterprise must address. Events are usually triggers or are triggered by something else: for example, an alert is a trigger ("X *must* occur"), or a notification is triggered ("X *has* occurred"). There are four general categories of Events: Arrival Events, Scheduled Events, Conditional Events, and Discovered Events. Arrival Events are driven by external forces such as "an order is placed." Scheduled Events are driven by dates and times, such as "end of year occurs."

Conditional Events are driven by specific criteria having been met, such as "invoice has gone unpaid for thirty days." Discovered Events are events of interest that cannot be predicted, such as "employee quits."

The following table provides examples of each type of Event:

Event Type	Examples
Arrival Event	• Received Order
	• Received Returned Product
Scheduled Event	• Ship order
	• End of Month
Conditional Event	• Low inventory threshold exceeded
	• Customer > 90 days late on payment
Discovered Event	• Employee quits
	• Raw materials do not arrive on time

Figure 4.11 – Event Types and Examples

Review and Approval

After the Planning Team works with the Core Business Team to create a final set of Roles, Locations, and Event models, the Executive Review Team should review and approve them as they do all other Enterprise Architecture Models.

Summary

The objective of the enterprise modeling phase is to achieve organization-wide consensus on the Goals, Processes, Materials, Roles, Locations, and Events that support the business now and those that are required to support future business. These models will be used, along with the systems inventory, to develop the target architecture. They will also be used to scope and determine the relative priority of projects.

The starter models created during the project preparation phase are used to kick off all of the modeling sessions. It is best if the Executive Review Team reviews and approves the models at the end of each modeling session. This approach reduces rework because the Core Business Team can incorporate feedback earlier in the process of developing the Enterprise Architecture.

To streamline communication, the Planning Team may need to partition a complicated model into a master model with submodels. Different diagrams with different levels of detail may need to be created for different audiences (these should be labeled as submodels to avoid confusion). The rendering needs to suit the audience.

CHAPTER 5

SYSTEMS INVENTORY

Overview

The systems inventory phase is the third phase of the Pinnacle Methodology for Enterprise Architecture. The purpose of the systems inventory is to identify and assess the organization's systems and to develop an understanding of the degree and quality of the automation it uses. In this context, "system" refers to any combination of software or hardware that is used to automate the Processes required to support the organization. Some organizations refer to the systems inventory as the application inventory or configuration management database.

The systems inventory phase can be started before the enterprise modeling phase is complete. During this phase, systems are usually mapped to the Processes, Materials, and the Roles they support. Doing this in parallel with the enterprise modeling phase can aid and refine the Processes and Materials Enterprise Architecture Models, but do consider resource constraints and timelines when deciding how much to parallelize activities.

The systems inventory will be used during the enterprise model analysis phase to analyze gaps, overlaps, and quality of service issues, as well as to provide an Application Asset Inventory. Consideration can be given to Processes, Materials, or Roles that are not currently supported by systems but could be candidates for mechanization. Overlaps are Processes that are supported by multiple systems. Analyzing overlaps can lead to substantial organizational technology savings through removal of redundant applications and their supporting infrastructure. The analysis may also uncover legitimate reasons to segregate materials in a certain manner or show that different systems are required to support different organizations. Since these types of analyses cannot be completed without the systems inventory information, the Planning Team should focus on inventorying systems during the system inventory phase and perform additional analyses once the Enterprise Architecture effort is completed.

Scoping the Inventory

The level of detail in the systems inventory should be consistent with the level of detail in the Process models. If the Processes are modeled at a high level, the inventory will concentrate on major systems. If there is a very detailed set of Processes, the inventory may be granular to contain individual modules from application suites. Regardless of how they are sourced, the inventory should include all systems used to support processes performed by the enterprise. Include homegrown applications, open source code, commercial off-the-shelf software, application service providers (ASPs), cloud services, and software used in support of outsourced process.

A question may arise regarding every database and spreadsheet in the possession of business personnel. Make explicit statements about whether or not these classes of systems are included in the Enterprise Architecture effort. A good rule of thumb to use is that if the system, mechanism, spreadsheet, or database is used as a basis for business decision making, it should be included in the analysis. If adequate time and resources have been allocated to the project, include process control systems, infrastructure components, integration software, decision support systems, reporting systems, and integrations in the systems inventory. In most companies, these systems account for the majority of the technology budget (aka the "shadow" information technology budget). Also include software that is licensed but not installed; it is common for a large company to purchase multiple site licenses for the same system. Uncovering these opportunities for cost reduction can have a direct impact on the financial bottom line. Make sure that any savings are attributed to the Enterprise Architecture planning project so that people understand the value of Enterprise Architecture planning!

Once the breadth and depth of the systems inventory is defined, you'll need to define the information requirements. Some organizations have hundreds of attributes in their systems inventory. When deciding which attributes to include, remember that it takes time to collect, enter, validate, and maintain each attribute.

The following list includes the minimum attributes to include in the systems inventory. The last three will be finalized when the enterprise modeling phase is complete:

- System name: Use the system name that the organization uses and spell out acronyms. System names should be unique.

- System description

- Hardware, operating system, and database platform

- Technologies and programming languages

- Internal business and technology owner

- External owner (vendor, service provider, outsourcer)

- Cost of ongoing support and maintenance

- Processes, Materials, and Roles supported

- Quality of the application from the business perspective

- Technical quality from the development, support, and operations perspective.

- Vision-enabling quality from the architecture perspective

Before starting the systems inventory process, check if the Governance, Security, or Data Center Operations group has a systems inventory you can leverage. If not, you can start with inventories from your enterprise program management office (PMO), compliance efforts such as Sarbanes-Oxley, or various development organizations. One of the positive outcomes of the "Y2K" debacle and Sarbanes-Oxley efforts is that they forced companies to start developing an understanding of the systems that support their business. Existing inventories can be leveraged to draft assessments even if they are not current.

The business owner and the Core Business Team should review the assessments regardless of how the information is compiled. The business may be using a myriad of homegrown systems that are not presently in an inventory. For example, the technology office may be very happy with the way a system is running, but the system may not meet actually meet the business requirements as defined by business personnel. It is not uncommon for a technology organization in even a midsize company to invest tens of millions of dollars (or for a large multinational corporation to invest hundreds of millions of dollars) in systems to support their business partners. If these different perspectives are not considered, the business gets frustrated and creates a creeping-mass mix of tools, spreadsheets, and manual processes it actually uses to run. The business stops talking to the technology office because it doesn't think that the technology office is listening to its concerns.

Streamlining the Process

When planning the systems inventory activity, consider that most large companies routinely have thousands of systems. Allocating a half day to each system means it would take many thousands of hours to assess the systems in a large company. Therefore, it is critical to try to leverage existing inventories, enlist the help of the technology development office and support organizations, establish data collection standards, and ensure that data is collected in a consistent fashion.

The following divide-and-conquer process could be used to streamline the task of identifying systems and completing system assessments:

1. Have each member of the Planning Team assemble a list of a particular business area's systems. The list should include key information such as system name, description, business owner, and technology point of contact.

2. Have one person collect the lists, combine them into one consolidated view of all business areas, and eliminate duplicates.

3. Conduct a brainstorming session to review and update the consolidated list.

4. Divide up the systems under review and decide when to meet and review the results. The person driving the inventory should use at least weekly checkpoints to monitor progress.

5. Work with the business and technology owners to complete the assessments that were assigned to them.

6. Reconvene and review the results.

To expedite the process, the Planning Team can enlist the aid of developers, analysts, and support personnel who are already familiar with the systems. If the Planning Team delegates some parts of the inventory to other teams, it is still responsible for the quality of the information and the completion of the inventory. If the primary technology point of contact does not have enough information to draft the assessment, the Planning Team member assigned to the system should harvest the information from existing documentation (e.g., system requirements, technical specifications). Once the assessment is drafted, review it with the technology and business points of contact.

When the Planning Team reconvenes, it should review the assessments for consistency. For example, the team should review the vision and quality ratings to ensure that they were applied consistently. Creating a system assessment template, with associated education, training, and sample assessments, will streamline the systems inventory process. The template can be a physical form, a spreadsheet, or a web page.

Here is an example of a physical form:

SYSTEM ASSESSMENT FORM	
SYSTEM NAME: MAINTENANCE REPORTING SYSTEM	
DESCRIPTION: THIS SYSTEM PROVIDES INFORMATION ABOUT MAINTENANCE ACTIVITIES IN AN ONLINE, QUERY-DRIVEN ENVIRONMENT. THE SYSTEM PULLS DATA FROM THE MAINTENANCE SCHEDULING SYSTEM INTO A DB/2 DATABASE AND MAKES IT AVAILABLE FOR ONLINE REVIEW AND REPORT GENERATION.	
Processes Supported: Maintain Equipment Manage Transactions	Materials Supported: Equipment Markets Packages Finances

Date Installed:
     07/09/2006
	Ongoing Cost:
	     $338,000/year

Language:
     Cobol
	Data Store
	     DB/2

Technical Quality
 	
     √ High   ☐ Medium
     ☐ Low
 	
 (Rate how well the system operates from a technical perspective)	

Customer Quality
 	
     ☐ High   √ Medium
     ☐ Low
 	
 (Rate how well the system supports process and requirements)	

Vision-enabling Quality
 	
     ☐ High   √ Medium
     ☐ Low
 	
 (Rate how well the system will support the future business vision described by the enterprise model)	

Assessed By: Mary Davis	Date: 03/05/2012

Figure 5.1 – Minimal System Assessment Example

After the systems inventory is complete, system diagrams can be created. The following example depicts the components and subcomponents of a financial management system.

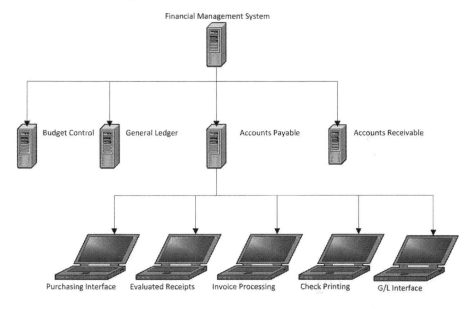

Figure 5.2 – System Component Diagram

Summary

If there are sufficient resources, the systems inventory can be started before the enterprise models are complete. The systems inventory will be used during the enterprise model analysis phase to refine the target architecture and scope projects. For example, if there are several systems that perform the same Process, a project may be established to consolidate the systems. Systems inventory is a valuable task outside of Enterprise Architecture. It provides an inventory of systems, which are valuable assets that the Enterprise needs to manage.

CHAPTER 6

ENTERPRISE MODEL ANALYSIS

Overview

In the enterprise modeling phase, the Architecture Work Group identified and described the Processes, Materials, Roles, Locations, and Events required to support the mission and Goals of the organization in its future state. They also identified the Processes, Materials, Roles, Locations, and Events that currently support the enterprise Goals. In the systems inventory phase, the Planning Team worked with business and technology partners to assess and document how well the current systems support the enterprise. The enterprise model analysis phase uses the enterprise models and systems inventory to define and refine the target architecture and identify the projects required to transform the enterprise to reach its desired future state.

In the enterprise model analysis phase, you will first develop Implementation Models that identify associations between the Architecture Models' artifacts. The Implementation Models are used to analyze the relationships between the Goals, Processes, Materials, Roles, Locations, Events, and systems. There are many types of Implementation Models, but decades of Enterprise Architecture practice enables us to suggest a set of Implementation Models that are most immediately valuable.

The first Implementation Model is used to determine which Processes support which Goals of the organization. The second represents the relationship between Materials required by each Process so that it is performed correctly. The third Implementation Model is used to determine which Processes have been automated—and how many times. This model is the relationship between Processes and systems. The fourth Implementation Model is used to determine what organizational Roles are required to perform each Process, and possibly, which Processes are not supported by any work efforts.

By combining the Processes-to-Goals Implementation Model and the Processes-to-Roles Implementation Model, the team can identify which work efforts are traceable to which Goals. The team will start to discover how Enterprise Architecture can increase productivity and reduce costs by identifying and eliminating work efforts that do not directly support the business Goals. The analysis can be sensitive, because some people will learn that their organization is wasting resources on Processes and Materials that are no longer optimal in the business environment. Explicit representations that are traceable and verifiable are the key to this understanding.

After the Implementation Models are developed, an affinity analysis algorithm is used to identify candidate projects or initiatives. Used in mathematical sciences for decades, the process is used to group Goals, Processes, Materials, Roles, Locations, Events, and other Enterprise Architecture attributes if modeled, such as systems. The Planning Team combines the outputs of the affinity analysis with the Implementation Models and systems inventory to refine the initiatives and projects. Once it has scoped the projects, it adds supplemental information to each one. The Core Business Team is critical to this process, because its members possess a deep understanding of the business and industry.

An initiative has many uses. Segmenting the Enterprise Model into manageable work units—units that may include candidates for automation or mechanization—is one kind of initiative. The initiative can be used as a risk analysis tool or as an unintended-consequences analysis tool. Each initiative defines the artifacts of the Enterprise Architecture Model that need to be considered when a change is contemplated to one or more artifacts. For example, within an initiative, one can see the dependencies of Goals, Processes, Materials, Roles, Locations, Events, systems, etc., and analyze the effect that a change in one artifact may have on other artifacts before the change is actually made. So, if a Goal is in the initiative and the executive team is considering a change to that Goal, an analysis can determine the effect of the Goal's change on Processes, Materials, and so on. If a business unit is considering a change to Process, an analysis can determine which Goals, Materials, Roles, Locations, and Events may be associated with the Process change. In other words, nothing in the enterprise stands alone. The concept of "transparent" changes in large enterprises without analysis has been shown to be fraught with danger. The Pinnacle Enterprise Architecture Methodology provides this extremely valuable analysis tool to the enterprise, helping it avoid unintended consequences.

The steps required to complete the enterprise model analysis phase are depicted in the following diagram. The rest of the chapter contains detailed information about each step.

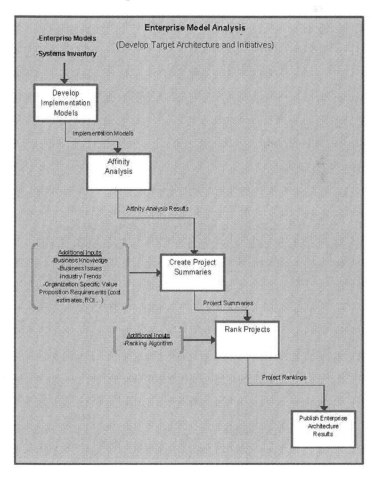

Figure 6.1 – Enterprise Model Analysis

Build Implementation Models

During this activity, the Planning Team and the Core Business Team create a series of Implementation Models to represent the associations of key enterprise aspects. The initial set of suggested Implementation Models are those used to represent the Processes required to support the Goals, the Materials required to support the Processes, the systems used to automate the Processes, and the Roles required for each process. Any two architecture artifacts can be related to form new insight into the organization.

In the next step, the relationships identified in the Implementation Models will be used to scope projects and ensure that the correct architecture artifacts are included in the analysis. Accurately identifying relationships is a key to reducing costs and improving quality of the enterprise itself and its associated systems. Without this type of analysis, it is fairly common for a project to go off track, because the team did not have the ability to analyze the impact of Processes, Materials, Roles, Locations, and Events contained within the initiative until after the solution was developed—much too late to take remedial actions. Once again, this analysis is an extremely valuable tool the enterprise can use as a direct result of Enterprise Architecture.

When creating the Implementation Models, the team should use a consistent level of granularity in each model. If the team uses the third-level Processes for the first Implementation Model, they should use the third-level Processes for the other Implementation Models. The team should also make sure that the Enterprise Architecture artifacts are at the same level of granularity. Some architects believe that only the lowest-level objects should be included in the analysis. Others believe that higher-level objects should be used for Enterprise Architecture planning and that more detailed levels should be left to the implementation teams. If the team is unsure, it should start with the third level across all artifacts and progress to more detailed levels if it needs to clarify relationships. The more granular the analysis, the less risk to the enterprise, but the more time is initially required. Tradeoffs need to be analyzed.

The Pinnacle Enterprise Architecture Methodology suggests that Processes be used as the "anchor" enterprise artifact, since most business personnel think along Process lines.

The Pinnacle Methodology focuses on these fundamental relationships required to understand the enterprise:

1. Processes support Goals

2. Processes require Materials

3. Processes are performed at Locations

4. Processes involve Roles

5. Processes are mechanized by systems

Building the Implementation Models is not technically difficult, but it is time-consuming and requires analytical skills. The team will need to create the Implementation Models and assess each relationship between the artifacts. There is no tool that can do the analysis for you; it requires human thinking and recognition, though a tool *can* help you "drive through" the large number of associations and record the results of your teams' analyses. Once these analyses are completed, the essence of the enterprise will be explicitly represented.

Processes-Support-Goals Implementation Model

The first association to analyze is which Processes are required to achieve Goals. The best way to represent this Implementation Model is to create a matrix that lists the Goals along one axis and the Processes along the other. The Implementation Model will be developed in the same manner that the Architecture Models were: the Planning Team develops the first model from traceable sources, and the refinements should be created in a working session with representatives from the Planning Team and the Core Business Team. If there are a lot of relationships (this is very likely), the team should form subteams and divide the work. The team can use sticky notes, flip charts, or a spreadsheet in the working session. If team members use flip charts or sticky notes, they should capture the information in a spreadsheet at the end of this step.

The Planning Team should use the Processes from the Enterprise Architecture Models to begin work on Implementation Models. This step will also help identify updates that should be incorporated in the Enterprise Architecture Models. The team should develop both Current As-Is-State and target Desired-State models, because—for example—a Process may appear in the current architecture even though the team may have eliminated it when they created the target architecture. Yet, the Implementation Model may show that the Process is still required for other reasons.

Start with the first Goal and review each Process to determine if it supports the Goal. Progress through the Goals until each Process's relationship to each Goal has been analyzed. Each relationship needs to have a traceable path to ensure that all people reviewing the analysis can see how and why the relationship is of importance. Proceed to the next Process until all possible relationships have been assessed. Keep the approach as simple as possible. Make Yes/No decisions and use an "X" to indicate a relationship. Do not assess the strength of a relationship yet—it complicates the work.

Use the following guidelines to evaluate the importance of an association between, for example, a Goal and a Process:

- Indicate a relationship if the Process plays a significant role in achieving the Goal.

- Do not indicate a relationship if the Goal can be completed without the Process.

- The degree of significance is determined by how well the Goal can be met without the Process being performed.

The Processes-Support-Goals relationships for the Sky High Gliders project are represented in the following model. The Process and Goal names are from the Enterprise Architecture Models in the enterprise modeling chapter. This Implementation Model represents the second-level (more detailed level) Goals and Processes, and the representations are grouped for better understanding.

Figure 6.2 – Processes-to-Goals Implementation Model

Processes	1.1 Double Number of Instructors	1.2 Open Kauai Operations	1.3 Increase Promotions by 40%	1.4 Expand Adventures by 50%	1.5 Return Fair Profit	2.1 Achieve 40% Repeat Business	2.2 Increase Pilot Flexibility	2.3 Publish Certification Handbooks in 2014	2.4 Achieve Zero Lesson Complaints	2.5 Expand Flying Tours	3.1 Increase Glider Usage by 25%	3.2 Develop Multi-Lesson Package	3.3 Decrease Equipment Failures	3.4 Re-qualify All Equipment	3.5 Institute Education Requirements
1 Manage Equipment															
1.1 Plan Equipment Needs		X		X	X					X	X				
1.2 Acquire Equipment		X		X						X	X		X		
1.3 Maintain Equipment						X						X	X		
1.4 Retire Equipment											X		X		
2 Sell Lessons															
2.1 Receive Customer Leads			X	X							X				
2.2 Propose Lessons		X		X		X	X				X				
2.3 Qualify Pilots				X				X					X	X	
2.4 Book Students											X				
3 Develop Markets															
3.1 Manage Locations	X	X				X	X	X							
3.2 Conduct Promotions	X	X	X			X						X			
3.3 Manage Agent Accounts	X	X				X						X			
3.4 Develop Market Forecasts						X				X					
4 Develop Adventures															
4.1 Analyze Customer Preferences		X				X	X	X		X					X
4.2 Receive Market Forecasts					X		X								
4.3 Design Adventures		X			X		X			X					X
4.4 Measure Adventure Satisfaction						X	X			X					
4.5 Make Adventure Improvements						X	X								
5 Conduct Certifications															
5.1 Prepare Lesson Plans						X			X						
5.2 Outfit Students						X			X						
5.3 Process Departures						X									
5.4 Process Certification Completions						X		X				X		X	
6 Manage Human Resources															
6.1 Develop Staffing Plans	X	X			X										
6.2 Acquire Employees	X	X		X	X			X							X
6.3 Assess Employee Performance						X									
6.4 Develop Education Programs	X				X										
6.5 Train Employees	X														
6.6 Terminate Employees												X			
7 Manage Finances															
7.1 Manage Transactions												X			
7.2 Manage Capital	X	X											X		
7.3 Manage Risks													X	X	X
7.4 Develop Budgets	X	X	X												
7.5 Monitor Policy Compliance															
7.6 Provide Financial Information	X	X										X			

If a consistent level of granularity was used, the Implementation Model will indicate the relative importance of each Process. Some of the findings and analysis of the model are:

- The "7.5 Monitor Policy Compliance" Process is not associated with any Goals. The team should investigate whether the Process is actually required. Since the description indicates that it is used to monitor compliance of internal policies, it does not appear to support regulatory requirements. A Goal should be created if it is required to correct a management concern. If it is not required, it should be removed from the target architecture.

- Since the remaining processes are associated with at least one Goal, they should be included in the target architecture.

- There does not appear to be any duplicate Process.

- Work efforts appear to be associated with each Goal since all of the Goals are associated with at least one Process.

- The team should investigate why the "1.1 Double Number of Instructors" Goal Name is not supported by any of the "2.0 Sell Lessons" or "5.0 Conduct Certifications" Processes. Three of four Processes under "3.0 Develop Markets" are associated with Goal 1.1; there are marketing activities associated with the Goal, but no sales or operations activities.

If a Goal is not supported by any Processes, do not assume that it can be removed from the Implementation Model. Such a disconnect may indicate a problem with the models, the analysis, or the enterprise itself. The Goal could actually be a "platitude." In addition, repeating patterns indicate a problem with the analysis. If a particular Goal is associated with every Process, you may subconsciously be trying to make the Process associated with the work efforts appear more important than it is. This is why the analysis needs traceability to written materials and should not be based on quick discussions or top-of-mind reviews. Be careful not to incorporate perceptions, personal opinions, or emotions in the analysis. Having a Planning Team do the analysis and not just an individual can reduce such potential pitfalls.

If the models and analysis are correct, make note of the issues and review them with the Core Business Team. One possible conclusion may be that someone needs to investigate the issues further and new Processes may need to be established. Make sure that the appropriate decision makers are aware of the issues raised and addressed as a result of the Enterprise Architecture planning project. This will underscore the importance and value of Enterprise Architecture planning.

Processes-Involve-Materials Implementation Model

The next association you will analyze determines what Materials are required for a Process to be performed. As with the previous Implementation Model, the best way to proceed is to create a matrix that lists the Processes on one axis and the Materials on the other. Develop the Implementation Model in the same manner as you developed the Architecture Models: the Planning Team develops the first model from traceable sources and the refinements should be created in a working session with representatives from the Planning Team and the Core Business Team. If there are a lot of relationships, the team should form subteams and divide the work. As with the prior Implementation Model, if the team uses sticky notes or flip charts, the information should be captured in a spreadsheet at the end, because the resulting Implementation Model will be the source for the affinity analysis later in the Methodology.

The Planning Team should use the Processes from the Enterprise Architecture Models to begin this step, which will also help identify updates to incorporate in the Enterprise Architecture Models. The team should develop both current As-Is-State and target Desired-State models.

After this Implementation Model is created, the team should analyze each Material in sequence to determine what Materials each Process needs to be correctly performed. The resulting Implementation Model will be used later in this phase to scope and prioritize the projects.

Use the following guidelines to determine if there is a significant relationship between a Material and a Process:

- Indicate a relationship if the Material is directly used in the Process.

- Do not indicate a relationship if the Process can be performed without the Material.

The Process-Involve-Materials relationships for the Sky High Gliders project are represented in the following Implementation Model. The Implementation Model represents the second-level Processes and Materials. The top levels of each Enterprise Architecture artifact are used to group objects and clarify relationships. The Process and Material names are from the examples in the enterprise modeling chapter.

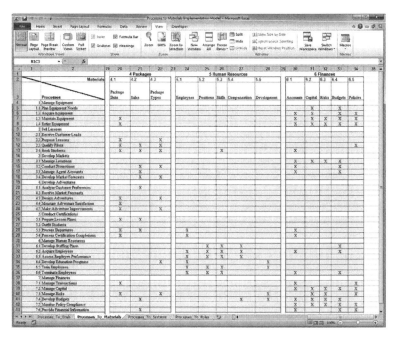

Figure 6.3 – Process-Involve-Materials Implementation Model

Figure 6.4 – Process-Involve-Materials Implementation Model (continued)

If a consistent level of granularity was used, the Implementation Model can be used to determine the relative importance of Materials in the performance of Processes. Some analyses and observations from the Implementation Models are:

- Every Material supports multiple Processes.

- Every Process—except "4.2 Receive Market Forecasts"—requires multiple materials.

- The "1.6 Equipment / Maintenance" Material is not associated with any human resources process. (The team should look at the human resources Processes to determine if they should be staffing or training people to maintain the equipment. They should also check if a problem with equipment maintenance indicates a problem with the performance of the individual or company that did the maintenance. Maintaining equipment properly is critical to this type of business. It reduces costs, increases safety, extends the life of critical equipment, and improves customer satisfaction. Conclusion: Further analysis is in order.)

Do not assume that a Material is not important and can be removed if it is not required by any of the Processes. Such a disconnect could, once again, indicate a problem with the models. If the models are correct, make note of the issue and review it with the Core Business Team.

Processes-Are-Mechanized-by-Systems Implementation Model

The next Implementation Model example analyzes how well the current systems support the existing business Processes. Again, create a matrix that lists the Processes along one axis and the systems are along the other. The system names will come from the systems inventory. Some systems are application suites that can be subdivided into systems or modules. For application suites, focus on components that can be licensed, purchased, or implemented separately. For example, Accounts Payable is a component system for a Financials or an Enterprise Resource Planning application suite. As with the other Implementation Models, the Planning Team develops the first model from traceable sources and the refinements should be created in a working session with representatives from the Planning Team and the Core Business Team; follow the aforementioned Implementation Model work and session suggestions.

Use the following guidelines to determine if a system supports a Process:

- Indicate a relationship if the system currently automates/mechanizes the Process.

- If a system enhancement is under way, evaluate the relationship as if the enhancement were already completed.

- Do not indicate a relationship if the enhancement is not funded.

- One test for whether a process is mechanized (computerized) is to answer the question, "Can the Process be performed without the system?"

The Processes-Are-Mechanized-by-Systems relationships for the Sky High Gliders example are represented in the following Implementation Model. The models and descriptions are from the examples in the enterprise modeling chapter.

Processes	01 Agent Reward Compensation System	02 Customer Scheduling System	03 Customer Evaluation Collection	04 Finance Reporting System	05 General Ledger	06 Maintenance Reporting System	07 Maintenance Scheduling System
1 Manage Equipment							
1.1 Plan Equipment Needs							
1.2 Acquire Equipment							X
1.3 Maintain Equipment						X	X
1.4 Retire Equipment							X
2 Sell Lessons							
2.1 Receive Customer Leads			X				
2.2 Propose Lessons			X				
2.3 Qualify Pilots							
2.4 Book Students			X				
3 Develop Markets							
3.1 Manage Locations	X						
3.2 Conduct Promotions							
3.3 Manage Agent Accounts							
3.4 Develop Market Forecasts							
4 Develop Adventures							
4.1 Analyze Customer Preferences		X					
4.2 Receive Market Forecasts							
4.3 Design Adventures			X				
4.4 Measure Adventure Satisfaction							
4.5 Make Adventure Improvements			X				
5 Conduct Certifications							
5.1 Prepare Lesson Plans		X					
5.2 Outfit Students		X					
5.3 Process Departures		X					
5.4 Process Certification Completions		X	X				
6 Manage Human Resources							
6.1 Develop Staffing Plans							
6.2 Acquire Employees							
6.3 Assess Employee Performance							
6.4 Develop Education Programs							
6.5 Train Employees							
6.6 Terminate Employees							
7 Manage Finances							
7.1 Manage Transactions	X	X		X	X	X	
7.2 Manage Capital				X	X		
7.3 Manage Risks							
7.4 Develop Budgets				X	X		
7.5 Monitor Policy Compliance							
7.6 Provide Financial Information				X	X		

Figure 6.5 – Processes-Are-Mechanized-by-Systems Implementation Model

116

Some of the observations from the Implementation Model are:

- All systems support at least one Process.

- None of the six human resources Processes are automated. The business will need to determine whether automating human resources Processes is a priority.

- The business will need to determine whether any of the following Processes should be automated. Marketing appears to be the biggest gap.

  ○ 1.1 Plan Equipment Needs

  ○ 2.3 Qualify Pilots

  ○ 3.2 Conduct Promotions, 3.3 Manage Agent Accounts, or 3.4 Develop Market Forecasts

  ○ 4.2 Receive Market Forecasts or 4.4 Measure Adventure Satisfaction

  ○ 7.3 Manage Risks or 7.5 Monitor Policy Compliance

Do not assume that a system can be eliminated if it does not support any of the Processes. First, validate the accuracy of the systems inventory and enterprise models. If no issues are found, review the issues with the Core Business Team. The team may find that the organization is spending time and money supporting a system that is not being used. Make sure that the Enterprise Architecture planning project is credited with identifying these issues and that the cost savings are attributed to the project as well.

Do not automatically assume you have identified an opportunity to implement a system if a Process is not supported by any systems. First, review the systems inventory and enterprise models for accuracy. Then, discuss the apparent gap with the Core Business Team. The team may find that there are business issues that can be addressed by automating the Process, or they may find that the Process does not need to be automated.

Processes-Involve-Roles Implementation Model

The next example Implementation Model to be analyzed is the relationship between Processes and Roles. You'll leverage this Implementation Model later in the Enterprise Architecture development Process to determine which Roles are involved in each move-ahead project and initiative. If the Roles are being restructured, or a restructuring is being planned, this Implementation Model can be used to assess possible impacts. For example, this Implementation Model is commonly used when an organization is moving to a Process focus or when new Process requirements arise within the organization.

As with the other Implementation Models, build a matrix listing the Roles along one axis and the Processes along the other. Develop it in the same manner that you developed the Architecture Models: the Planning Team develops the first model from traceable sources and the refinements should be created in a working session with representatives from the Planning Team and the Core Business Team. Follow the guidance on developing the model as suggested in the prior Implementation Model discussions. In most cases, there will only be a current set of Roles. If there are multiple versions, we always recommend that the team should start with the target desired-state architecture.

Representatives from the Planning Team and Core Business Team should then validate and update the Implementation Model in a working session.

Use these guidelines to identify the Processes-Involve-Roles relationships:

- Only indicate an association if the Role has a direct involvement in that Process.

- Indicate a relationship if at least one person in the organization performs the Role as part of the Process.

- One test for a relationship is "can the Process be performed without the Role?"

- If planned or proposed organizational changes were included in the Implementation Model, highlight them.

The Processes-Involve-Roles relationships for the Sky High Gliders project are represented in the following Implementation Model. The Process and Role names are from the examples in the enterprise modeling chapter.

Processes	01 Lesson Operations	02 General Manager	03 Finance & Administration	04 Human Resources	05 Information Technology	06 Maintenance	07 Marketing & Promotions	08 Sales	09 Certification Operations
1 Manage Equipment									
1.1 Plan Equipment Needs		X					X		
1.2 Acquire Equipment						X			
1.3 Maintain Equipment						X			
1.4 Retire Equipment						X			
2 Sell Lessons									
2.1 Receive Customer Leads								X	
2.2 Propose Lessons							X	X	
2.3 Qualify Pilots								X	
2.4 Book Students	X		X	X				X	X
3 Develop Markets									
3.1 Manage Locations		X	X				X		
3.2 Conduct Promotions							X		
3.3 Manage Agent Accounts							X		
3.4 Develop Market Forecasts							X		
4 Develop Adventures									
4.1 Analyze Customer Preferences									
4.2 Receive Market Forecasts									
4.3 Design Adventures	X	X					X	X	X
4.4 Measure Adventure Satisfaction									
4.5 Make Adventure Improvements									
5 Conduct Certifications									
5.1 Prepare Lesson Plans	X								X
5.2 Outfit Students									
5.3 Process Departures									
5.4 Process Certification Completions	X								X
6 Manage Human Resources									
6.1 Develop Staffing Plans		X	X	X	X				
6.2 Acquire Employees				X					
6.3 Assess Employee Performance	X	X	X	X	X	X	X	X	X
6.4 Develop Education Programs	X	X	X	X	X	X	X	X	X
6.5 Train Employees									
6.6 Terminate Employees		X		X					
7 Manage Finances									
7.1 Manage Transactions			X						
7.2 Manage Capital			X						
7.3 Manage Risks									
7.4 Develop Budgets	X	X	X	X	X	X	X	X	X
7.5 Monitor Policy Compliance									
7.6 Provide Financial Information		X	X		X				

Figure 6.6 – Processes-Involve-Roles Implementation Model

Some of the observations from the Implementation Model are:

- Every Role is associated with multiple Processes.

- Nine subprocesses are not associated with any Roles. Therefore, the Core Business Team should review and update the Implementation

Model. There may be some missing associations, Roles, or Processes. There may also be some Processes that are no longer required. The subprocesses that are not associated with any Roles are:

- ○ 4.1 Analyze Customer Preferences, 4.2 Receive Market Forecasts, 4.4 Measure Adventure Satisfaction, 4.5 Improve Adventures

- ○ 5.2 Outfit Students, 5.3 Process Departures

- ○ 6.5 Train Employees

- ○ 7.3 Manage Risks and 7.5 Monitor Policy Compliance

Affinity Analysis

The Pinnacle Enterprise Architecture Methodology uses affinity analysis as the first step in defining the initiatives and projects required to transform the enterprise. The major objective of affinity analysis is to stratify or segment the planning information collected in the prior phases. You can then make informed decisions about which projects to undertake. Affinity analysis is an important tool for making such decisions because it brings together relevant business information in an easy-to-analyze form.

Affinity analysis groups Enterprise Architecture artifacts together based on common associations (relationships) between them. Affinity analysis determines the degree of likeness, or affinity, between pairs of objects, and then uses that affinity as a basis for grouping Enterprise Architecture artifacts with common characteristics. For example, grouping together Processes that use the same Materials is an affinity analysis. A candidate project is then initially defined as a group of Processes that have a defined affinity for the same Materials. Affinity analysis can also be used to group Goals based on common Processes, to group Processes based on common Roles, and to group organizations based on any other common artifacts that are identified within Enterprise Architecture.

Affinities are determined by calculating the ratio of the number of associations two objects have in common compared to the number of associations they *could* have in common. The result is expressed as a percentage.

For example, two Materials that are always involved with the same Process have an affinity of 100 percent. Two Materials that are not involved with any of the same Processes have an affinity of 0. If the two Materials are involved with the same Processes half of the time, they have an affinity of 50 percent. Next, Processes are grouped into projects based on the calculated affinities. Object pairs with high affinities, as compared to specific thresholds, form the basis for each group. The remaining objects are assigned to the initial groups based on calculated, weighted affinities.

The affinity analysis operates under two basic assumptions. First, artifacts are represented in the enterprise models. Second, associations between objects have been represented in Implementation Models. Since Process is the anchor object, the affinity analysis uses the relationships in the Processes-to-Materials Implementation Model to identify candidate projects. Supplemental information from the Implementation Models will be added to the resulting projects. The projects' priority, risk, funding, and person-month estimates for implementation can also be estimated.

Some technology teams propose projects solely based on feedback from stakeholders. They get a list of wants or desires, generate requirements definitions, and start developing. This is not architecture; it is implementation, no matter what models are built. In the Pinnacle Enterprise Architecture Methodology, the candidate projects are developed from the Architecture and Implementation Models and are then used to generate ideas and collect feedback from the Core Business Team and Executive Review Team. This approach enables the team to objectively consider the strategic needs of the organization rather than focus on implementations that may or may not be required. It also facilitates cross-organizational buy-in, since the candidate projects are created using statistical methods rather than feedback from a limited number of stakeholders.

Performing Affinity Analysis

This section may seem to be more about math than about strategy. We concur! We want to offer you an opportunity to understand the mathematical basis of the affinity analysis, but you can skip this section if you're not interested.

To show how affinity analysis is performed using an Implementation Model, we use the example here of the Processes-Require-Materials

Implementation Model: the projects are created by grouping together Processes according to common Material usage.

The following variables control the grouping algorithm:

- *Minimum affinity to form a new group.* This threshold ratio is used for grouping together two Processes. If Processes have an affinity of less than this value, they are not grouped.

- *Minimum affinity to merge groups.* This threshold ratio is used for merging two groups into one.

- *Minimum affinity to add an object to a group.* This threshold ratio is used for adding an object to an existing group.

- *Minimum affinity to consider objects at all.* Processes whose affinity falls below this value will not be grouped together.

How Enterprise Architecture Artifacts Are Grouped

The variables listed above control the grouping algorithm. If the team is unfamiliar with performing affinity analysis, it should start with the initial recommended values provided with the EACOE tool. In general, if higher affinity values are specified for the variables, two objects must be more similar to be placed in the same group.

The algorithmic steps listed here reference Processes, the anchor object, to add clarity:

1. Calculate the affinity value for each Process pair by following this sequence:

   a. Divide the number of Material associations that the *first* Process has by the number of Material associations that the first and second Process share.

   b. Divide the number of Material associations that the *second* Process has by the number of Material associations the first and second Process share.

   c. Divide the sum of steps (a) and (b) by 2. The yield is the average affinity for this Process pair.

2. Rank the Process pairs from highest to lowest according to their affinity values.

3. Group the Processes based in their affinities using the following logic.

    a. If neither Process is already in a group, and if their affinity is greater than or equal to the value selected for the "Minimum affinity to form a new group" parameter, a new group is created. Otherwise, a new group is not created.

    b. If just one of two Processes is in a group, and if their affinity is greater than or equal to the value selected for the "Minimum affinity to add an object to a group" parameter, then the second Process is added to the group. If not, the second Process is not added to the group.

    c. If the Processes are in different groups, and if their affinity is greater than or equal to the value selected for the "Minimum affinity to merge groups" parameter, then the groups are combined.

    d. If either Process was not added to a group, add it to the "Miscellaneous" group.

    e. This algorithm can easily be mechanized, and its complexity hidden, with a product like Microsoft Excel, the vehicle for the EACOE tool.

Affinity Analysis Results

The primary output of the affinity analysis is a list containing Process groups. The analyst can monitor the algorithm and report out what was calculated for each Process pair. This will provide some guidance on how to adjust the variables, if required. For example, if the affinity analysis creates too many small groups, the "Minimum affinity to form a new group" parameter may be low. If in the first cycle the affinity analysis places all of the Processes in a single group, the "Minimum affinity to add an object to a group" may be too low.

Here is a sample processing report. Descriptions of each column follow.

Cycle	Process	Pair	Affinity	Action
1	1.3	1.4	95%	Create
2	1.2	1.3	79%	
3	1.1	1.2	73%	
4	1.1	1.4	69%	
5	1.2	1.4	68%	
6	1.1	1.3	67%	

- **Cycle:** The first Process pair is analyzed in Cycle 1, the second in Cycle 2, and so on.

- **Process Pair:** Lists the two Processes that were analyzed in respective cycles. "1.3 Maintain Equipment" and "1.4 Retire Equipment" were analyzed in the first cycle.

- **Affinity:** Lists the averaged affinity value for the Process pair.

- **Action:** Describes what the affinity analysis did with this Process pair. The possible actions are "Create" (create a group), "Merge" (merge two groups), "Add" (add the object[s] to a group) and "Bypass" (place the object[s] in the miscellaneous group).

For a small number of Processes, the analysis can be done manually. The algorithm will need to be automated for a large organization with hundreds or thousands of Processes. For instance, a programmer with Microsoft Excel experience should be able automate the affinity analysis algorithm fairly quickly using his or her favorite tools and programming language.

Outputs of the Affinity Analysis

The outputs of the affinity analysis for the Sky High Gliders Enterprise Architecture planning project are shown below. These outputs include the affinity matrix, the usage matrix, and the Process grouping report. The usage matrix is a summary of the associations between pairs of Processes. The only difference between the affinity matrix and the usage matrix is that the affinity matrix shows the affinity values and the usage matrix has an 'X' in place of the affinity value.

	Processes	1 Manage Equipment			
		1.1	1.2	1.3	1.4
Processes		Plan Equipment Needs	Acquire Equipment	Maintain Equipment	Retire Equipment
1	Manage Equipment				
1.1	Plan Equipment Needs	■	73%	67%	69%
1.2	Acquire Equipment	73%	■	79%	68%
1.3	Maintain Equipment	67%	79%	■	95%
1.4	Retire Equipment	69%	68%	95%	■

Figure 6.7 – Usage Matrix

	Processes	1 Manage Equipment			
		1.1	1.2	1.3	1.4
Processes		Plan Equipment Needs	Acquire Equipment	Maintain Equipment	Retire Equipment
1	Manage Equipment				
1.1	Plan Equipment Needs	■	X	X	X
1.2	Acquire Equipment	X	■	X	X
1.3	Maintain Equipment	X	X	■	X
1.4	Retire Equipment	X	X	X	■

Figure 6.8 – Affinity Matrix

Initiative 1 contains Processes:
3.4 Develop Market Forecasts
4.3 Design Adventures
4.5 Improve Adventures

Initiative 2 contains Processes:
1.3 Maintain Equipment
1.4 Retire Equipment
7.3 Manage Risks
7.5 Monitor Policy Compliance

Initiative 3 contains Processes:
1.2 Acquire Equipment
3.1 Manage Locations
7.2 Manage Capital

Initiative 4 contains Processes:
5.1 Prepare Lesson Plans
5.2 Outfit Students

Initiative 5 contains Processes:
7.1 Manage Transactions
7.6 Provide Financial Information

Initiative 6 contains Processes:
6.1 Develop Staffing Plans
6.2 Acquire Employees
6.3 Assess Employee Performance
6.6 Terminate Employees

Initiative 7 contains Processes:
6.4 Develop Educational Programs
6.5 Train Employees

Initiative 8 contains Processes:
2.1 Receive Customer Leads
2.2 Propose Lessons

Initiative 9 (not grouped) contains Processes:
1.1 Plan Equipment Needs
2.3 Qualify Pilots
2.4 Book Students
3.2 Conduct Promotions
3.3 Manage Agent Accounts
4.1 Analyze Customer Preferences
4.2 Receive Market Forecasts
4.4 Measure Adventure Satisfaction
5.3 Process Departures
5.4 Process Certification Completions
7.4 Develop Budgets

Figure 6.9 – Process Grouping Report

Affinity Analysis Follow-Up

Once the affinity analysis is complete, the team will need to review the groupings to decide whether to adjust variables and rerun the affinity analysis or use the groupings to form projects. At minimum, the final results should be used to make sure all of the impacted Enterprise Architecture components are reviewed when defining the scope of each implementation project. Commonality of Materials may be the only factor to consider when creating technology-facing projects, but there may be business-specific reasons why two Processes sharing the same Materials should be distributed into separate projects. In those cases, move Processes from one project to another and document the criteria for that decision.

Creating Candidate Projects

After the Process-grouping affinity analysis is performed, the Core Business Team works with the Planning Team to create and refine candidate projects based upon the generated list of initiatives. Don't do this without the Core Business Team's active review; you need the depth and breadth of its knowledge about the company or industry. Enterprise Architecture is about business understanding before technology planning. The business experts may merge projects to minimize dependencies or split a large project into one or more independent projects. It is also not uncommon for the team to propose additional projects. In fact, the initiatives generated by the Process groupings from affinity analysis can spur innovation that has a significant impact on the organization.

Use the following steps to create a list of candidate projects from the algorithmic generation of initiatives:

1. Select a candidate initiative to develop from the Process grouping report.

2. List the Processes that were grouped together on a blank initiative summary grid.

3. Add the Materials, Goals, Roles, Locations, Events, and systems related to each Process. (This information can be found in the Implementation Models you previously developed.)

4. Based on the team's knowledge of the business, industry trends, and new innovations, identify the Processes that should move from the list of ungrouped, "bypassed" Processes or from another initiative to this initiative. Maintain traceability for these decisions.

5. Add the Materials, Goals, Roles, Locations, Events, and systems related to each of the newly added Processes.

6. Create a meaningful initiative name and summary description.

7. Document significant dependencies (e.g., another initiative, a pending merger).

8. Address the value proposition. (See below for more information on this.)

9. Research issues and update the initiative summary.

10. Document open issues related to the initiative—for example, which members of the Executive Review Team are likely to oppose the initiative and/or its projects, and why. Review these issues with the Executive Sponsor in preparation for the review and verification phase.

Articulating the Value Proposition

Formal costing and return-on-investment calculations are outside the scope of this book, but the Executive Review Team will need to understand the value proposition for each initiative so it can determine which initiative projects to fund. The value proposition should include rough estimates of the initiative projects' costs and benefits to the organization. The approach to developing estimates will vary depending on the type of project. The team can contact colleagues in the organization or at other companies to find out how much was invested in similar projects. Alternatively, it can propose a proof of concept or solution-definition project that the organization will fund before it moves forward with an implementation project.

Sample Initiative Definition

In the following example, the Processes identified in the affinity analysis are shown. The Processes, Materials, and Goals highlighted were added by the Core Business Team as a result of moving two of the Processes from the ungrouped list to Initiative 8. The other Enterprise Architecture Artifacts that make up the initiative come from the Implementation Models.

Initiative 8: Customer Satisfaction		
This initiative will evaluate a current customer lead and match it against the customer's skills and preferences. The resulting adventure package will reflect what the customer has requested, based on customer's ability to safely participate in the glider adventure.		
Processes Included	**Materials Required**	**Goals Supported**
2.1 Receive Customer Leads 2.2 Propose Lessons 2.3 Qualify Pilots 4.1 Analyze Customer Preferences	2.1 Customer Data 2.2 Preferences 3.3 Agents 4.1 Package Data 4.2 Sales 4.3 Package Types 6.5 Policies	1.1 Double Number of Instructors 1.2 Open Kauai Operations 1.3 Increase Promotions by 40% 1.4 Expand Adventures by 50% 1.5 Return Fair Profit 2.1 Achieve 40% Repeat Business 2.2 Increase Pilot Certification Flexibility 2.3 Publish Handbooks in 2009 2.5 Expand Flying Tours 3.1 Increase Glider Usage by 25% 3.3 Decrease Equipment Failures 3.4 Pre-qualify All Customers 3.5 Institute Education Requirements
Roles Impacted	**Locations Impacted**	**Systems Impacted**
07 Marketing & Promotions 08 Sales		02 Customer Scheduling
Significant Dependencies		
None		
Value Proposition		
Resource requirements include $500,000 and 12 man-months. After the first year, revenue is expected to increase 5% per year due to repeat business.		

Figure 6.10 – Initiative Summary

Prioritizing Initiatives

After the initiatives are scoped, the Planning Team establishes the relative priority of each initiative using an objective and logical approach. Criteria to consider include Goal alignment and initiative dependencies. Before settling on a process, the Planning Team should check whether the organization has standard criteria or calculations.

Here are two approaches to ranking initiatives:

Approach 1

This approach prioritizes initiatives based on business Goal alignment. The process is easy to understand, and it uses information gathered earlier in this phase.

The steps for this approach are:

1. *Assign relative weights to the Goals in the Goal model.*

   Use a relative ranking system to account for the fact that any two Goals can be equally important. The example shown in Figure 6.11 uses a relative ranking system of 1–5, where 5 identifies critical Goals.

2. *Calculate scores for higher-level Goals by averaging sub-Goal rankings.*

   The scores are averaged because summing the Goals would skew the analysis toward Goals with a higher number of sub-Goals.

3. *After scoring the Goals, calculate the initiative rankings based on how well they support the Goals.*

   As in the example in Figure 6.12, create a table that lists the Processes included in the project in the first column and the Goals that support each Process in the second column (these are from the Processes-to-Goals Implementation Model.) List the score beside each Goal and the subtotal of the Goal scores for each Process. Calculate the initiative score by averaging the subtotals.

4. *Prioritize the initiatives based on this aggregated Goal score.*
Higher scores indicate higher priority.

Goal Name		Score
1.0	Become Market Leader	3
1.1	Double Number of Instructors	5
1.2	Open Kauai Operations	4
1.3	Increase Promotions by 40%	3
1.4	Expand Adventures by 50%	2
1.5	Return Fair Profit	1
2.0	Satisfy Customers	3.2
2.1	Achieve 40% Repeat Business	5
2.2	Increase Pilot Certification Flexibility	1
2.3	Publish Handbooks in 2009	3
2.4	Achieve Zero Lesson Complaints	5
2.5	Expand Flying Tours	2
3.0	Maximize Returns	4.2
3.1	Increase Glider Usage by 25%	5
3.2	Develop Multi-Lesson Package	2
3.3	Decrease Equipment Failures	5
3.4	Pre-qualify All Customers	5
3.5	Institute Education Requirements	4

Figure 6.11 – Goal Relative Ranking Scores

Process Name	Goals Supported	Score
2.1 Receive Customer Leads	1.3 Increase Promotions by 40%	3
	3.1 Increase Glider Usage by 25%	5
	Sub-Total:	8
2.2 Propose Lessons	2.1 Achieve 40% Repeat Business	5
	3.1 Increase Glider Usage by 25%	5
	Sub-Total:	10
2.3 Qualify Pilots	3.3 Decrease Equipment Failures	5
	3.4 Pre-qualify All Customers	5
	Sub-Total:	10
4.1 Analyze Customer Preferences	1.1 Double Number of Instructors	5
	1.2 Open Kauai Operations	4
	1.4 Expand Adventures by 50%	2
	1.5 Return Fair Profit	1
	2.1 Achieve 40% Repeat Business	5
	2.2 Increase Pilot Certification Flexibility	1
	2.3 Publish Handbooks in 2009	3
	2.5 Expand Flying Tours	2
	3.5 Institute Education Requirements	4
	Sub-Total:	27
	Total	55
Initiative Aggregate Goal Score (55 / 4 processes rounded up):		14

Figure 6.12 – Project Score

Approach 2

If multiple criteria are used, the team will need to decide how to weight each criterion. The following example shows how to modify the calculation to prioritize the initiatives based on how well the Goals are supported and how well the Processes are automated in today's environment. The example uses an automation score, which is a composite of the quality ratings that were assigned during the systems inventory phase.

The approach is:

1. Calculate the Average Process/Goal Score

2. Calculate the Average Process/Automation Score

3. Use this formula to calculate the score for each initiative:

[80% * average Process/Goal score] + [20% * average Process/automation score]

Documenting the Enterprise Architecture

In this task, the Planning Team generates the final Enterprise Architecture documents for the present iteration: the executive summary, the initiative descriptions, and the overall Enterprise Architecture Model information.

Develop the Executive Summary

The purpose of the Executive Summary is to give decision makers enough information to determine which initiatives to fund and implement. The Project Lead creates the report. All members of the Architecture Work Group, and the executives who influence funding decisions, will review it.

The Summary usually contains:

*   **Introduction.** Presents a high-level overview of the Enterprise Architecture project. Includes the objectives of Enterprise Architecture and lists the team members.

- **Conceptual Overview.** Presents a brief overview of the Pinnacle Enterprise Architecture Methodology and the approaches used to model the enterprise, inventory the systems, analyze the models, and create and rank the initiatives.

- **Gantt (Sequence) Chart.** Indicates dependencies between initiatives and subprojects over the planning time frame:

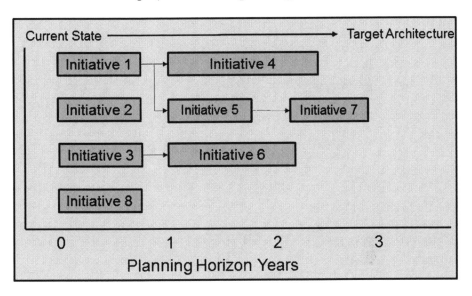

- **Initiative List.** Straightforwardly lists initiatives and subprojects and includes the number, name, and description for each initiative and project.

- **Initiative Ranking Graph.** Illustrates the relative priority of each initiative and subproject in a graph format:

Become Market Leader	
Satisfy Customers	
Market / Prod. Develop.	
Accounting / Financial Ctrl	
Improve Employee Perform.	

- **Initiative Summaries.** Provide brief understandings of the attributes of the initiatives.

- **Common Questions.** Includes anticipated questions and proactively answers them.

Detailed Initiative Descriptions

Support each initiative summary with a detailed initiative description that includes the concepts behind the initiative and the information that was used to estimate funding. Also include more detailed information about each Process, Material, Goal, Role, Event, Location, and system impacted in the initiative. The Executive Sponsors may want to review some of the detailed descriptions prior to the initiative prioritization meeting. The implementation team may also want to review them as part of the required analysis transition.

Overall Enterprise Model Report

The overall enterprise model report is a consolidation of all the information developed during the Enterprise Architecture project. The report includes the names, descriptions, and models for each of the Enterprise Architecture components. It also includes the Implementation Models that were created in the enterprise model analysis phase.

Summary

During the enterprise modeling analysis phase, the Planning Team works with the Core Business Team to verify the integrity of the desired-state/target architecture by creating a series of Implementation Models that relate Processes to Goals, Materials, and Roles. Then, statistical methods (affinity analysis) are used to identify candidate initiatives. The Planning Team works with the Core Business Team to refine the initiatives based on knowledge of conditions beyond the mathematical algorithms. After the team reaches consensus on the Enterprise Architecture-driven initiatives, the initiatives are ranked against support of Business Goals and strategies and sequenced according to their relative priority and dependencies.

The Planning Team creates the executive summary, detailed Enterprise Architecture project documentation, and enterprise model documentation before moving on to the review and verification phase.

CHAPTER 7

REVIEW AND VERIFICATION

Overview

The objective of the review and verification phase is to finalize the move-ahead initiative scoping and initiative ranking and to decide on next steps. At the end of this phase, one or more initiatives will be selected for implementation based on available funding, initiative rankings, and initiative dependencies. After the initiatives are selected, an Executive Sponsor is selected for each approved initiative. During the analysis transition phase, project teams are formed to implement each of the selected initiatives. Members of the Architecture Work Group will be assigned to each initiative to transfer their knowledge to the move-ahead teams and to make sure that each initiative continues to stay aligned with the Enterprise Architecture.

Pre-Meeting Communications

During this phase, the executive summary is presented to the Executive Sponsor and each member of the Executive Review Team, usually in one-on-one meetings. After the meetings, the Executive Sponsor works with the

Executive Review Team to resolve issues that may have arisen. Members of the Planning Team and Core Business Team should be available to answer questions and research issues. The Executive Review Team may need to review detailed project documentation and rescope some of the initiative. The initiative prioritization meeting is held after the issues raised are resolved, and the required changes are identified and addressed.

Meeting Preparation

A member of the Planning Team should facilitate the initiative prioritization meeting. Prior to the meeting, the facilitator should work with the rest of the Planning Team to try to anticipate questions, mitigate issues, and prepare the agenda. This should be a face-to-face meeting held in an environment that enables the Executive Review Team to focus on the task at hand. This means providing advance notice, arranging travel, clearing schedules, and providing refreshments.

Initiative Prioritization Meeting

The objective of the initiative prioritization meeting is to finalize the move-ahead initiatives, select initiatives for implementation, and position the initiatives for success. At the beginning of the meeting, the facilitator should review the meeting agenda and objectives. The facilitator should leverage the executive summary, since it is designed to facilitate this meeting. First, review the introduction and overview with attention to the planning process and target architecture by highlighting the approach used to develop the initiatives, the various teams that participated, and the differences between the Enterprise Architecture initiative approach and past project development approaches.

Discuss the move-ahead initiatives, rankings, and dependencies along with the agreed-upon changes. The meeting minutes should make note of those changes so that the Enterprise Architecture artifacts and associated materials can be updated. After the move-ahead initiatives and rankings are finalized, the Executive Review Team should discuss the available funding and decide which initiatives to implement.

If the Executive Review Team cannot decide which initiatives to fund, the team may want to provide a voting mechanism. With Enterprise Architecture, this is an approach that works well, since the initiative development approach, Enterprise Architecture process, and models are now explicit. The votes can be applied to a single initiative or spread across multiple initiatives. After tallying the votes and seeing the results, team members have an opportunity to advocate for any specific initiative before making the final decisions.

Common Issues to Avoid

Not Staying Objective

The Planning Team needs to stay objective during this meeting. The Enterprise Architecture is not their property: they are the architects, not the owners. If initiatives are re-scoped and re-ranked, the facilitator should document in the meeting minutes what changed, who requested the change, and the rationale for making the change.

Analyzing Decisions in the Meeting

Regardless of how close the Planning Team is to the process, the initiative prioritization meeting is not the place to backtrack through the analysis. If members of the Executive Review Team question the analysis, log their questions but investigate them outside of the meeting.

Summary

The purpose of the review and verification phase is to select the move-ahead initiatives to fund and implement. Once the Executive Review Team finalizes the initiatives, rankings, and next steps, a member of the team is selected to sponsor each approved initiative. The Planning Team should update the initiative documentation at the end of this phase to keep the Enterprise Architecture evergreen.

CHAPTER 8

ANALYSIS TRANSITION

Overview

The objective of the analysis transition phase is to make sure that the organization reaps the benefits of the Enterprise Architecture planning project. In the prior phases, a series of explicit representations were developed that describe the enterprise in terms of its Goals, Processes, Materials, Roles, Locations, Events, and systems. After analyzing the explicit representations, the team scoped the initiatives required to transform the enterprise to its desired state. In the review and verification phase, the executives reviewed and approved the desired state/target architecture, approved the initiatives to be implemented, and selected an Executive Sponsor for each initiative.

The major tasks involved in the analysis transition phase are to:

1. Develop and implement the transition plan.

2. Marshall the initiatives through the analysis transition phase.

3. Institutionalize governance of the desired state/target architecture and implementation.

If there are significant dependencies between initiatives, the Planning Team will need to work with the organization's project managers, to manage the dependencies. If the initiatives were scoped properly, the project manager responsible for each implementation should be able to manage the dependencies between initiatives.

Transition Plan

The Planning Team is responsible for developing and executing the transition plan, which includes continuing education and training, establishing modeling and analysis standards, and partnering with the implementation teams. This section explains the first two components, while the third is discussed in the initiative transition and analysis section with respect to each initiative.

Education

The first objective of the transition plan is to make key members of the organization aware of the desired-state/target architecture and the approach used to implement the Enterprise Architecture. This helps ensure that each implementation team has cross-organizational representation and that key decision makers participate in the appropriate initiative. This activity will be accomplished through executive briefings, "lunch and learns," audio conferences, and webcasts.

At the end of this activity, the Enterprise Architecture planning project deliverables will have been widely distributed and reviewed with key members of the organization. Stakeholders will be aware that the Enterprise Architecture was developed with input from the entire organization, and that it represents the stated Goals and direction of the organization as communicated in a series of explicit models and model details. Gone are the thousand pages of text! These communications should minimize, if not eliminate, initiatives and behaviors that could undermine the implementation of the strategic direction of the enterprise.

Analysis and Modeling Standards

The second objective of the transition plan is to ensure that a consistent set of analysis methods and techniques is used across implementation teams. The enterprise modeling standards defined in the project preparation phase should be reviewed and updated to reflect the organization's current standards. The resulting standards must be easy to learn and implement. Implementation teams will need to be trained in modeling techniques before proceeding with the analysis.

The Planning Team should also make sure any required tools are available to members of the implementation teams and that the implementation teams have been trained in how to use the tools. However, if the organization does not have any Enterprise Architecture tools, the initiative implementations should not be put on hold while the Planning Team evaluates, selects, purchases, installs, and configures them. A good time to review tool options might be after the first Enterprise Architecture project is performed.

Initiative Transition and Analysis

Executive Sponsorship

If the Enterprise Architecture has already been integrated into the corporate governance processes, the Executive Review Team was able to finalize initiative prioritization and funding in the review and verification phase. If not, the Executive Sponsor for each initiative will need to secure funding. After the initiative is funded, the Executive Sponsor will need to establish the implementation team. At least one person from either the Planning Team or Core Business Team should be assigned to each initiative. You must assume that changes will be required, especially early on in Enterprise Architecture maturity.

Planning Team and Core Business Team

Members of the Architecture Work Group are responsible for marshaling the implementation teams through the analysis transition phase, and hopefully through full implementation. They should compile a transition portfolio for each initiative, host an initiative kickoff meeting, and conduct initiative-specific modeling and analysis activities. These work efforts are intended to facilitate integration and alignment between implementation initiative and the Enterprise Architecture. At the end of the analysis transition phase, representatives from the Planning Team should update the Enterprise Architecture materials and models with information from the implementation initiative.

Initiative Transition Documents

An initiative transition document is required for each initiative. These documents are used to convey the information from the Enterprise Architecture planning project that each implementation team needs. They are also used to control the scope of implementation initiative, support integration of multiple initiatives, and provide a starting point for developing additional models used for system implementation. The Architecture Work Group representative assigned to each initiative is responsible for compiling the initiative transition document from the documentation developed in the prior phases.

The first component of the initiative transition document is an introduction. The introduction presents an overview of the Enterprise Architecture planning project, the role of the initiative transition document, and a summary of the contents. The second component is an identification of each Goal and a definition for each Goal the initiative supports. The third component, at a minimum, is an identification of all of the Processes and Materials and a definition for each Process and Material that defines the boundaries of the initiative. The fourth component is a list of Roles, Locations, and Events impacted by the initiative. The last component is the list of systems that will be impacted by the initiative.

Initiative Kickoff Meeting

The initiative transition document is used to conduct the initiative kickoff meeting. The Architecture Work Group representative is responsible for scheduling the kickoff meeting, developing the agenda, and distributing the initiative transition document. The Architecture Work Group representative is also responsible for working with the initiative's Executive Sponsor on pre-meeting communications. The representative may choose to facilitate the kickoff meeting or enlist a trained facilitator.

During the first part of the meeting, the implementation team is introduced to the Enterprise Architecture methodology, initiative approach, and deliverables. Then, the Architecture Models, Implementation Models, and system inventory information that describe the current/baseline architecture and desired-state/target architecture are reviewed with the implementation team. After the team understands the target architecture, they should discuss the initiative's summaries. This approach ensures that the implementation team understands how its initiative relates to other initiatives that are being undertaken, the target architecture that is to be implemented, and how other projects that are currently underway will be coordinated.

The next thing to do in the meeting is to use the initiative transition document to guide discussion of the actual initiative being undertaken. Once the implementation team understands the scope and objectives of the initiative, it discusses the deliverables, roles, responsibilities, and next steps. The next steps may include additional knowledge transfer and education. The team may decide to break the initiative into smaller subprojects and form subteams. If so, the team needs to clearly define the boundaries of the subprojects and make sure that they are aligned and integrated.

By the end of the initiative kickoff meeting, the implementation team should be familiar with the initiative and how it relates to the Enterprise Architecture. It should also have a plan that includes refining the initiative scope, identifying updates to the Enterprise Architecture, and creating models required for the specific initiative.

Initiative Analysis

Implementation Models

The Processes-to-Roles Implementation Model is used to refine the initiative scope and ensures that the correct organizations are participating in the initiative. The Processes-to-System Implementation Model is used to refine the initiative scope and to ensure that the business and technology owners of the impacted systems are involved in the initiative.

Post-Analysis Transition Activities

The modeling and analysis efforts discussed in this chapter represent the activities required to complete the analysis transition phase. Most organizations will specify additional activities in their project life cycle. Activities may include finalizing the detailed requirements, selecting the operating platform, and finalizing the technical design. Since these additional activities can change the initiative direction and boundaries, the last steps in the analysis transition phase are to integrate architecture governance into existing corporate governance structure and to update the Enterprise Architecture Models.

Institutionalize Governance

This section discusses corporate governance from the perspective of the Enterprise Architecture planning project. Governance is an important topic that addresses legal and regulatory compliance, balancing the needs of the organization's stakeholders (e.g., shareholders, employees, suppliers, and customers), fiduciary responsibility, and accountability. It includes the structures, processes, and policies that determine how decisions are made, how compliance is monitored, how performance is measured, and how individuals are motivated. The specifics of how an organization should implement governance are outside the scope of this book.

Existing governance mechanisms should be leveraged to ensure that:

1. Initiatives and projects are implemented in a way that is consistent with the approved Enterprise Architecture.

2. Exceptions are only approved when there is a significant business justification and resultant modifications to the Enterprise Architecture are noted.

3. The desired-state/target architecture is updated to reflect new Goals and requirements.

To be effective, Enterprise Architecture governance must be consistently applied across all business and technology projects. In a small-to-midsized organization, the activities described in the previous section may be sufficient to govern the construction and maintenance of the target architecture. More formal governance mechanisms are required in a large multinational corporation, a complex organization, or an organization that is undergoing rapid or significant change.

If it has not already been done, the Executive Sponsor should task a member of the Planning Team with implementing Enterprise Architecture governance at the beginning of the Enterprise Architecture planning project. The Enterprise Architecture planning process must be integrated into the existing initiative prioritization and funding mechanisms, and Enterprise Architecture checkpoints must be added to the project management methodology and sourcing Processes.

Initiative and Project Prioritization and Funding

In an ideal situation, the annual Enterprise Architecture planning project update and formal refresh would be considered a component of corporate governance, and it would be the only way to prioritize and fund a project. However, there are times when additional projects are required between planning cycles. This may be due to legal or regulatory requirements, a merger or acquisition, a change in the industry, or business requirements initially missed by the Enterprise Architecture planning project. At a minimum, answer these questions about any project proposed outside of the Enterprise Architecture:

1. Which enterprise Goals does this initiative or project support?

2. Does this initiative or project create new Processes?

3. How will this initiative or project impact existing Processes?

4. Will this initiative or project require any organizations to perform a Process that is already being performed by another organization?

5. Have the organizations responsible for the impacted Processes agreed to this initiative or project's proposed changes?

6. Will this initiative or project create additional systems?

7. Have the organizations that maintain the systems that support the impacted Processes assessed the impact of this proposed initiative or project?

8. Will this initiative or project create additional Materials?

9. How will this initiative or project impact existing Materials?

10. How are the systems and roles that maintain the Materials impacted by this initiative or project?

Once an initiative or project is approved, someone should be assigned to guide the project team through the analysis transition phase and update any of the affected architectures to reflect the new understandings. The guide should be someone who is already familiar with the Enterprise Architecture planning process and target architecture. If the business requirements have been considered in the Enterprise Architecture planning project, the cause of the gap should be identified, and it should be corrected in the next Enterprise Architecture planning project. For example, if the change was due to lack of participation by certain business units, additional or alternate representatives should be added to the Architecture Work Group.

Initiative Implementation

Most midsized-to-large organizations use a standard methodology to implement business and technology projects. They may call it the project life cycle, product life cycle, or software development life cycle. Business and technology projects should be reviewed at critical junctures to ensure that they align with the Enterprise Architecture. As time passes, members of the Architecture Work Group will become more focused on implementation tasks than on Enterprise Architecture alignment. Architecture Work Group members should stay with the initiatives through their implementation, not just through the Enterprise Architecture activities. Therefore, the initiative should be reviewed at the following junctures, if applicable:

1. The end of the analysis transition

2. Before executing a development agreement

3. Before executing an outsourcing agreement

4. Before a capital expenditure is approved

5. Before the solution is deployed.

Each of these reviews should confirm that the project is aligned with the Enterprise Architecture and that it does not conflict with another on-going project. The review should include the same questions that were assessed when the initiative was funded.

The organization may need to develop a scorecard to ensure that project teams use a consistent set of criteria to assess initiatives. In addition to providing a concise, systematic way to monitor and measure Enterprise Architecture compliance, a scorecard will provide the raw data required to monitor and report project trends. For example, it can be used to assess the value of marshaling implementation teams through the analysis transition phase.

Summary

The desired-state/target architecture needs to be implemented for the organization to reap the benefits of the Enterprise Architecture planning project. The target architecture is implemented through a series of initiatives. During the first part of the analysis transition phase, the Architecture Work Group focuses on developing and implementing the transition plan, which includes establishing modeling and analysis standards and positioning the initiatives for success by making the organization aware of the Enterprise Architecture components.

The second set of activities is associated with marshaling the implementation initiatives through the analysis transition phase. The team focuses on knowledge transfer, initiative-specific analysis, integration, and alignment. The last set of activities focuses on integrating Enterprise Architecture governance into existing governance mechanisms. The objective is to integrate checkpoints into project initiation, funding, sourcing, and the project implementation life cycle.

CHAPTER 9

ONGOING PLANNING

Overview

The Enterprise Architecture planning project defined the desired-state/target architecture and the series of initiatives and projects required to implement it. After the initiatives were approved and funded, the members of the Architecture Work Group transferred their knowledge to the implementation teams and conducted initiative-specific modeling and analysis activities. The objectives were to launch the initiatives, align them with the Enterprise Architecture, and construct a foundation that would facilitate reuse and integration.

Each implementation initiative will change the current architecture. The enterprise could be impacted by each initiative in several ways. For example:

- Business units, divisions, departments, or work groups could be reorganized.

- One or more Processes could be centralized, decentralized, or outsourced.

- Facilities could be consolidated or moved.

- One or more Processes could be automated.

- Material assets may be created or eliminated.

The enterprise will also be impacted by executive decisions, changes in the industry, new government regulations, technology innovations, and other initiatives. Therefore, we need a way to manage change.

Ongoing planning addresses how planning should be performed in the years that follow the initial Enterprise Architecture planning project. Ongoing planning has three objectives. First, the enterprise models need to be updated periodically to reflect changes as the business changes. Second, the Executives need to determine which additional initiatives and projects to fund. Third, the Executives need to determine if ongoing initiatives or projects should be stopped or redirected.

Enterprise Architecture planning is intended to supplement the budgeting processes. If the organization budgets on an annual basis, the Enterprise Architecture planning project should act as a gatekeeper to the annual budget. The rest of this chapter assumes an annual budget cycle because most organizations budget annually. However, the comments and processes apply equally to both more frequent and less frequent budgeting cycles.

Ongoing Updates

Some components of the Enterprise Architecture should be maintained between budgeting cycles. Responsibility for maintaining those components should be distributed throughout the organization. This approach will improve the accuracy of the models and institutionalize the Enterprise Architecture planning process. It will also shorten the duration of the annual Enterprise Architecture planning refresh project.

Ideally, the following components should be maintained by the following groups in the organization:

Goals

Corporate Planning should be responsible for the ongoing maintenance of the Goal models. In a large organization, Corporate Planning may act as the Goal model custodian and distribute responsibility for maintaining the models to department heads. As the custodian, Corporate Planning is responsible for the overall accuracy, currency, and consistency of the models. Maintaining a visual representation of the Goals makes it easier for executive management to ensure corporate Goals are supported by department Goals and individual work efforts. They will be able to identify and mitigate problems earlier in the year.

Processes

The current list of Processes and Process descriptions are ideally maintained by department managers. Since maintaining Processes within departments may cause duplication, the Process models will need to be reconciled as part of the annual Enterprise Architecture planning project, or a "Process custodian" may be assigned to each Process or set of Processes.

Materials

Materials descriptions and models are usually maintained by the "data" organization. This organization (which might also be called data management or enterprise information management) should also work with the implementation teams to ensure that the models are consistent and aligned.

Roles and Locations

Roles and Locations models are usually maintained by the Human Resources activity. If the Human Resources activity implements a system that distributes responsibility for maintaining Role and Location information, it becomes the custodian of this information and is therefore responsible for the integrity and quality of the models and descriptions.

Events

Event models are usually maintained by the business personnel who have the greatest stake or involvement in the Event. Because of the usefulness of Event modeling in providing business agility, event models are sometimes maintained in a "team" or "department" that actually spans the Enterprise itself.

Systems Inventory

The systems inventory is usually maintained by a technology organization. In a large technology organization, technology service management or technology operations may be responsible for the systems inventory. The Architecture Work Group should validate this information during the annual Enterprise Architecture planning project refresh, since some artifacts may not be maintained between planning cycles.

Annual Planning Project

The original Enterprise Architecture planning project probably took four to seven months. The exact duration varies with the complexity of the organization and the experience of the Planning Team. The duration of the annual Enterprise Architecture planning project refresh will also vary depending on how much the enterprise has changed since the last project. To minimize the learning curve, at least one member (but hopefully more) of the original Enterprise Architecture Planning team should be assigned to the annual planning project update.

Since the target architecture is developed based on the Goals, the target architecture should not change unless the Goals of the organization change. The architecture components associated with the enterprise model analysis are created to scope initiatives and determine which initiatives and projects to fund. So, the annual budgeting cycle is usually the only time the enterprise model analysis is required, and deliverables should only need updating during the annual planning project. If the target architecture and the projects change too frequently, the organization will not make progress toward its Goals. This usually indicates issues that may include Enterprise Architecture, but that probably indicate more serious organizational issues.

Situation Assessment

The Enterprise Architecture planning project refresh starts with a situation assessment, which is used to determine what has changed in the organization since the last Enterprise Architecture planning project. The current Goal, Process, Material, Role, Location, and Event names, descriptions, and models should be collected from the groups that have been maintaining them. If changes to models were tracked, the logs should be reviewed. If the changes were not logged, the current models should be compared to the baseline Architecture Models to ascertain the level of effort required to conduct the planning project refresh.

Project Management

Once the magnitude of the changes is understood, the Project Lead is ready to develop the project plan. You can leverage the checklists in appendix A to develop the initial Enterprise Architecture project plan as well as the Enterprise Architecture project plan refresh. The Project Lead should review the Enterprise Architecture repository and update the stakeholder analysis before kicking off the planning project refresh.

Enterprise Models

If the Goals, Processes, Materials, Roles, Locations, and Events models were not maintained, surveys and interviews can be used to identify changes to the baseline architecture. The stakeholder analysis should target a small group of individuals who can provide the required information. Use a workshop to review and finalize the models. If most of the team is familiar with the planning process, the workshop shouldn't take much time.

Systems Inventory

Create systems assessments based on the systems inventory. The business and technology owners should update the assessments before proceeding. The business owners should validate the quality of ranking criteria, ensuring that they have been maintained between planning projects.

Implementation Models and Initiatives

The enterprise model analysis tasks are required to determine the impact of the changes on the enterprise. After the Implementation Models have been updated and the initiatives have been scoped and ranked, reconcile the resulting initiatives with last year's initiatives. Ongoing initiatives that would not be recommended in light of the current Goals should be brought to the attention of the Executive Review Team. The Executive Review Team should review the progress of the initiatives against expectations, the impact on dependent initiatives, sunken or committed costs, and plausible return on investment. The final initiatives list will include recommendations to fund new initiatives, add funding to ongoing initiatives, rescope initiatives, stop work on initiatives, or eliminate funding for initiatives that were funded but not started.

Budget Process

If the review and verification phase is not part of the annual budgeting process, its resulting recommendations should be submitted to the budgeting process. The analysis transition phase starts after the initiatives are approved.

Challenges

Timing

The ongoing planning project team must allocate enough time to do an effective and high-quality job. Start the ongoing planning project refresh early enough to complete it before the beginning of the budgeting cycle.

Maintaining the Enterprise Architecture Artifacts

Keeping good records is always a challenge. Planning information needs to be documented and organized so that you can quickly and easily locate, understand, and reuse it.

Maintaining a Business Focus

There are three primary ways to maintain a business focus. First and foremost, make sure that the business actively participates in the planning project. Ideally, the business drives the project. Second, distribute ongoing Enterprise Architecture modeling activities to the appropriate organizations, if possible. Third, institutionalize the planning process so that it just happens.

Resource Management

Since the original Planning Team has the best understanding of the methodology, at least one person from last year's Planning Team should be assigned to the continuing planning project activity. This could be a consulting resource who is an expert in the process or a Planning Team member who has completed an Enterprise Architecture and implementation project.

Since ongoing Enterprise Architecture maintenance has hopefully been distributed throughout the organization, a relatively small, central Enterprise Architecture team may be sufficient. It is very difficult for people in a centralized Enterprise Architecture organization to maintain their relevance and expertise. The Planning Team and Core Business Team members were selected for their ability to deliver knowledge of the business and their modeling expertise. After the planning project, members of the Planning Team and Core Business Team should be assigned to implementation initiatives. This will help them maintain their expertise, learn new skills, and reap the benefits of their efforts. After successfully implementing one of the initiatives, they will have demonstrated that they can develop a complete Enterprise Architecture and deliver tangible results. This enhances everyone's value to the organization in a way that is clearly visible to executive management and expands their influence with their business and technology partners.

Summary

The objective of the Enterprise Architecture planning project is to define a desired-state/target architecture based on the organization's Goals and to identify the initiatives required to construct that architecture. Enterprise Architecture enables business strategy in a clear and unambiguous way. Once the target architecture is created and the initiatives have been scoped, they should be reviewed and updated as part of the annual budgeting process. To expedite the planning process and improve the quality of the deliverables, maintenance of the models, descriptions, and systems inventory should be distributed to corporate planning, human resources, and sourcing, or to vendor management, technology personnel, and business managers. Enterprise Architecture is the key component of Enterprise agility.

APPENDIX A:

PROJECT CHECKLISTS

Project Preparation Checklist

- ❏ 1.1 Initiate Project
  - ❏ 1.1.1 Secure Executive Sponsor
  - ❏ 1.1.2 Determine Scope and Objectives
  - ❏ 1.1.3 Secure Funding
  - ❏ 1.1.4 Identify Project Participants
  - ❏ 1.1.5 Discuss Project Schedule
  - ❏ 1.1.6 Document Project Plan
- ❏ 1.2 Train Potential Participants
  - ❏ 1.2.1 Recruit Enterprise Architecture Project Participants
  - ❏ 1.2.2 Conduct Planning Methodology Training
  - ❏ 1.2.3 Conduct Meeting Facilitation Training
- ❏ 1.3 Arrange Project Logistics
  - ❏ 1.3.1 Select Participants, Securing Commitments from Each Project Participant's Executive Level
  - ❏ 1.3.2 Discuss Arrangements for Geographically Dispersed Teams
  - ❏ 1.3.3 Arrange Facilities
  - ❏ 1.3.4 Acquire Supplies, Equipment, and Software

❏ 1.3.5 Establish Document Repository
❏ 1.3.6 Revise and Publish Project Schedule
❏ 1.4 Develop Initial Models
  ❏ 1.4.1 Define Modeling Conventions
  ❏ 1.4.2 Review Modeling Approach and Sample Deliverables
  ❏ 1.4.3 Gather source documents to harvest for Goal, Process, and Material Models
  ❏ 1.4.4 Develop Initial Goal, Process, and Material Models
  ❏ 1.4.5 Document Initial Models
❏ 1.5 Develop Communication and Acceptance Approach

  ❏ 1.5.1 Create Stakeholder Analysis and Stakeholder Action Plan
  ❏ 1.5.2 Create Communication Plan
  ❏ 1.5.3 Create Executive-Level Presentations

Enterprise Modeling Checklist

❏ 2.1 Conduct Architecture Orientation Meeting
  ❏ 2.1.1 Identify Audience Background and Perspective
  ❏ 2.1.2 Present Overview of Enterprise Architecture Planning Project
  ❏ 2.1.3 Educate Audience about Enterprise Modeling
  ❏ 2.1.4 Present Initial Model Case Study
  ❏ 2.1.5 Prepare for Workshop
❏ 2.2 Conduct Enterprise Model Workshop
  ❏ 2.2.1 Review Objectives and Agenda
  ❏ 2.2.2 Review Initial Models
  ❏ 2.2.3 Identify, Define, and Model Goals
  ❏ 2.2.4 Identify, Define, and Model Processes
  ❏ 2.2.5 Identify, Define, and Model Materials
  ❏ 2.2.6 Identify, Define, and Model Roles, Locations, and Events
  ❏ 2.2.7 Review and Assign Open Issues
❏ 2.3 Document Workshop Results
  ❏ 2.3.1 Review Workshop Notes
  ❏ 2.3.2 Document Definitions
  ❏ 2.3.3 Document Diagrams
  ❏ 2.3.4 Conduct Quality Assurance Review
  ❏ 2.3.5 Publish Workshop Results

Supplemental Interview Checklist

- ❏ 2.1 Prepare for Interviews
  - ❏ 2.1.1 Develop and Deliver Introduction
  - ❏ 2.1.2 Review Enterprise Architecture Planning Project Charter
  - ❏ 2.1.3 Develop Interview Process
  - ❏ 2.1.4 Review Initial Models
  - ❏ 2.1.5 Develop Thought-Starting Questions
- ❏ 2.2 Conduct Interviews
  - ❏ 2.2.1 Conduct Introduction and Overview
  - ❏ 2.2.2 Review Initial Models
  - ❏ 2.2.3 Review Thought-Starting Questions
  - ❏ 2.2.4 Summarize Interview Results
  - ❏ 2.2.5 Discuss Next Steps
- ❏ 2.3 Develop Interview Summaries
  - ❏ 2.3.1 Develop Introduction
  - ❏ 2.3.2 Recap Interview
  - ❏ 2.3.3 Revise Models
  - ❏ 2.3.4 Develop Next Steps
- ❏ 2.4 Consolidate Interview Summaries
  - ❏ 2.4.1 Develop Initial Consolidated Summary
  - ❏ 2.4.2 Identify and Document Concerns
  - ❏ 2.4.3 Investigate and Resolve Concerns
  - ❏ 2.4.4 Develop Consolidated Models
- ❏ 2.5 Conduct Review Meeting
  - ❏ 2.5.1 Review Introduction and Objectives
  - ❏ 2.5.2 Review Consolidated Models
  - ❏ 2.5.3 Identify Changes
- ❏ 2.6 Revise Consolidated Models

Systems Inventory Checklist

- ❑ 3.1 System Inventory Preparation
  - ❑ 3.1.1 Review Systems Inventory Process
  - ❑ 3.1.2 Identify Existing Inventories
  - ❑ 3.1.3 Create Initial List of Systems
  - ❑ 3.1.4 Identify Attributes Needed for Systems
  - ❑ 3.1.5 Create System Assessment Template
  - ❑ 3.1.6 Identify for Each System: Business Users and Information Technology (IT) Points-of-Contact
  - ❑ 3.1.7 Assign System Assessments to Team Members
- ❑ 3.2 Inventory Systems
  - ❑ 3.2.1 Gather and Review Existing Documentation
  - ❑ 3.2.2 Draft System Assessments
  - ❑ 3.2.3 Interview System IT Points-of-Contact
  - ❑ 3.2.4 Interview Business Users
  - ❑ 3.2.5 Update Systems Assessments
- ❑ 3.3 Document Inventory Results
  - ❑ 3.3.1 Review Ratings for Consistency
  - ❑ 3.3.2 Update System Inventory Information
  - ❑ 3.3.3 Publish Systems Inventory Results

Enterprise Model Analysis Checklist

- ❑ 4.1 Review Modeling Analysis Process
- ❑ 4.2 Develop Implementation Models
  - ❑ 4.2.1 Develop Processes-Supports-Goals Model
  - ❑ 4.2.2 Develop Processes-Uses-Materials Model
  - ❑ 4.2.3 Develop Processes-Are-Implemented-by-Systems Model
  - ❑ 4.2.4 Develop Processes-Involve-Roles Model
  - ❑ 4.2.5 Analyze Issues and Refine Results
  - ❑ 4.2.6 Document Implementation Models Results

❑ 4.3 Scope Initiatives
  ❑ 4.3.1 Create Processes Grouping Analysis (Affinity Analysis)
  ❑ 4.3.2 Refine Initiatives
  ❑ 4.3.3 Create Summaries for Initiatives and Their Projects
  ❑ 4.3.4 Identify Dependencies
  ❑ 4.3.5 Optionally Estimate Funding and Personnel Requirements
  ❑ 4.3.6 Optionally Estimate Return on Investment
❑ 4.4 Prioritize the Initiatives
  ❑ 4.4.1 Establish Ranking Criteria
  ❑ 4.4.2 Calculate Initiatives Rankings
  ❑ 4.4.3 Create Ranking Graph
❑ 4.5 Produce Final Documentation
  ❑ 4.5.1 Produce Executive Summary
  ❑ 4.5.2 Produce Detailed Initiatives Descriptions
  ❑ 4.5.3 Produce Overall Enterprise Model Report

Review and Verification Checklist

❑ 5.1 Conduct Pre-Meeting Communications
❑ 5.2 Address Issues
❑ 5.3 Identify Meeting Preparation and Logistics
❑ 5.4 Conduct Initiatives Prioritization Meeting
  ❑ 5.4.1 Review Planning Process
  ❑ 5.4.2 Review Executive Summary
  ❑ 5.4.3 Review Initiatives Summaries
  ❑ 5.4.4 Discuss Initiatives Dependencies
  ❑ 5.4.5 Discuss Issues and Proposed Changes
  ❑ 5.4.6 Discuss Available Funding and Options
  ❑ 5.4.7 Select Initiatives, Projects for Implementation
  ❑ 5.4.8 Select an Executive Sponsor for Each Initiative
❑ 5.5 Update Documentation

Analysis Transition Tasks Checklist

- ❑ 6.1 Prepare for Analysis Transition
  - ❑ 6.1.1 Conduct Enterprise Strategy Education
  - ❑ 6.1.2 Standardize Analysis Techniques
  - ❑ 6.1.3 Ensure Tools Are Available
  - ❑ 6.1.4 Create Integrated Initiative Projects Schedule
- ❑ 6.2 Establish Initiative Projects
  - ❑ 6.2.1 Secure Initiative Project Funding
  - ❑ 6.2.2 Build Implementation Team
  - ❑ 6.2.3 Develop Initiative Project Transition Documents
- ❑ 6.3 Conduct Initiative Project Kickoff Meetings
  - ❑ 6.3.1 Review Meeting Objectives and Agenda
  - ❑ 6.3.2 Review Enterprise Architecture Planning Project Methodology
  - ❑ 6.3.3 Review Executive Summary
  - ❑ 6.3.4 Review Project Transition Document
  - ❑ 6.3.5 Discuss Next Steps and Devise Plan
- ❑ 6.4 Conduct Initiative Project Analysis
  - ❑ 6.4.1 Refine Initiative Project Scope
  - ❑ 6.4.2 Identify Additional Initiative Project Participants
  - ❑ 6.4.3 Identify Updates to Enterprise Models
  - ❑ 6.4.4 Develop Additional Implementation Models (e.g., Business Process Models, Entity Relationship Models)
- ❑ 6.5 Institutionalize Governance
  - ❑ 6.5.1 Identify Initiative Project Prioritization and Funding
  - ❑ 6.5.2 Define Initiative Project Implementation Approaches
  - ❑ 6.5.3 Identify Sourcing and Purchasing Requirements

APPENDIX B:

PINNACLE'S QUICK START PROJECT PLAN

This section shows several snapshots of the Pinnacle Enterprise Architecture Quick Start Methodology Project Plan, expanded as needed to show the details of each major stage.

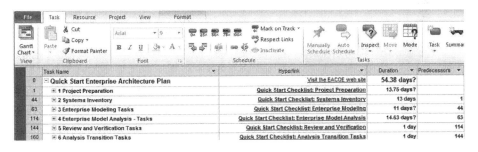

The detail of Project Preparation:

	Task Name	Hyperlink	Duration	Predecessors
0	⊟ **Quick Start Enterprise Architecture Plan**	Visit the EACOE web site	**54.38 days?**	
1	⊟ **1 Project Preparation**	Quick Start Checklist: Project Preparation	**13.75 days?**	
2	⊟ **1.1 Project Initiation Meeting**	EACOE's view of Enterprise Architecture	1 day	
3	1.1.1 Determine Project Objectives	Executive Sponsor Commitment	1 hr	
4	1.1.2 Determine Project Scope		1 hr	3
5	1.1.3 Identify Project Participants	Who makes a good team member?	1 hr	4
6	1.1.4 Determine Modeling Approach		3 hrs	5
7	1.1.5 Develop Initial Project Schedule		1 hr	6
8	1.1.6 Document Project Plan		1 hr	7
9	⊟ **1.2 Arrange Project Logistics**		4.5 days?	2
10	1.2.1 Recruit Project Participants	Architect Roles in an Enterprise	3.5 days	
11	1.2.2 Arrange Facilities		0.5 days	10
12	1.2.3 Acquire Equipment and Software		0.5 days	
13	1.2.4 Gather Source Documents for Harvesting	Quick Start Source Document Indices	1 day?	12
14	1.2.5 Develop Initial Inventory		2.5 days	13
15	1.2.6 Acquire Existing Business Plans		3.5 days	
16	1.2.7 Publish Revised Project Schedule		4 hrs	15,12,14
17	1.2.8 Initialize and share Normative Vocabulary Glossary	Quick Start Glossary Concepts	1 day?	
18	⊟ **1.3 Initial (Straw) Architecture Modeling**		7.25 days?	9
19	1.3.1 Present Planning Orientation		1 hr	
20	1.3.2 Review Existing Business Plans		1 hr	19
21	⊞ **1.3.3 Develop Initial Architecture Models**	EACOE Classification Reminder	6 days?	20
30	⊞ **1.3.4 Diagram Initial Architecture Models**		1 day?	29
38	1.3.5 Update Normative Vocabulary Glossary	Quick Start Glossary Concepts	1 day?	
39	⊟ **1.4 Pre-Technical Review**		1 day	18
40	1.4.1 Present Planning Methodology		1 hr	
41	1.4.2 Review Planning Sample Deliverables		3 hrs	40
42	1.4.3 Present Analysis Overview		1 hr	41
43	1.4.4 Discuss Planning and Analysis Transition		3 hrs	42
44	⊞ **2 Systems Inventory**	Quick Start Checklist: Systems Inventory	13 days	1
63	⊞ **3 Enterprise Modeling Tasks**	Quick Start Checklist: Enterprise Modeling	11 days?	44
114	⊞ **4 Enterprise Model Analysis - Tasks**	Quick Start Checklist: Enterprise Model Analysis	14.63 days?	63
144	⊞ **5 Review and Verification Tasks**	Quick Start Checklist: Review and Verification	1 day	114
160	⊞ **6 Analysis Transition Tasks**	Quick Start Checklist: Analysis Transition Tasks	1 day	144

The detail of Systems Inventory:

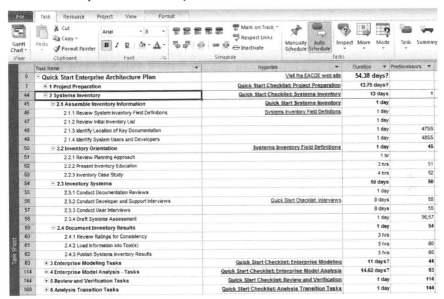

	Task Name	Hyperlink	Duration	Predecessors
0	Quick Start Enterprise Architecture Plan	Visit the EACOE web site	54.38 days?	
1	1 Project Preparation	Quick Start Checklist: Project Preparation	13.75 days?	
44	2 Systems Inventory	Quick Start Checklist: Systems Inventory	13 days	1
45	2.1 Assemble Inventory Information	Quick Start Systems Inventory	1 day	
46	2.1.1 Review System Inventory Field Definitions	Systems Inventory Field Definitions	1 day	
47	2.1.2 Review Initial Inventory List		1 day	
48	2.1.3 Identify Location of Key Documentation		1 day	47SS
49	2.1.4 Identify System Users and Developers		1 day	48SS
50	2.2 Inventory Orientation	Systems Inventory Field Definitions	1 day	45
51	2.2.1 Review Planning Approach		1 hr	
52	2.2.2 Present Inventory Education		3 hrs	51
53	2.2.3 Inventory Case Study		4 hrs	52
54	2.3 Inventory Systems		10 days	50
55	2.3.1 Conduct Documentation Reviews		1 day	
56	2.3.2 Conduct Developer and Support Interviews	Quick Start Checklist: Interviews	8 days	55
57	2.3.3 Conduct User Interviews		8 days	55
58	2.3.4 Draft Systems Assessment		1 day	56,57
59	2.4 Document Inventory Results		1 day	54
60	2.4.1 Review Ratings for Consistency		3 hrs	
61	2.4.2 Load Information into Tool(s)		5 hrs	60
62	2.4.3 Publish Systems Inventory Results		5 hrs	60
63	3 Enterprise Modeling Tasks	Quick Start Checklist: Enterprise Modeling	11 days?	44
114	4 Enterprise Model Analysis - Tasks	Quick Start Checklist: Enterprise Model Analysis	14.63 days?	63
144	5 Review and Verification Tasks	Quick Start Checklist: Review and Verification	1 day	114
160	6 Analysis Transition Tasks	Quick Start Checklist: Analysis Transition Tasks	1 day	144

The detail of Enterprise Modeling:

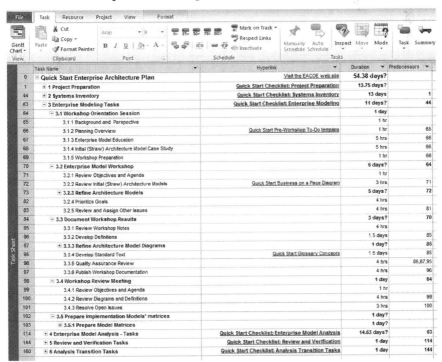

	Task Name	Hyperlink	Duration	Predecessors
0	Quick Start Enterprise Architecture Plan	Visit the EACOE web site	54.38 days?	
1	1 Project Preparation	Quick Start Checklist: Project Preparation	13.75 days?	
44	2 Systems Inventory	Quick Start Checklist: Systems Inventory	13 days	1
63	3 Enterprise Modeling Tasks	Quick Start Checklist: Enterprise Modeling	11 days?	44
64	3.1 Workshop Orientation Session		1 day	
65	3.1.1 Background and Perspective		1 hr	
66	3.1.2 Planning Overview	Quick Start Pre-Workshop To-Do template	1 hr	65
67	3.1.3 Enterprise Model Education		5 hrs	66
68	3.1.4 Initial (Straw) Architecture Model Case Study		5 hrs	66
69	3.1.5 Workshop Preparation		1 hr	68
70	3.2 Enterprise Model Workshop		6 days?	64
71	3.2.1 Review Objectives and Agenda		1 hr	
72	3.2.2 Review Initial (Straw) Architecture Models	Quick Start Business on a Page Diagram	3 hrs	71
73	3.2.3 Refine Architecture Models		5 days?	72
82	3.2.4 Prioritize Goals		4 hrs	
83	3.2.5 Review and Assign Other Issues		4 hrs	81
84	3.3 Document Workshop Results		3 days?	70
85	3.3.1 Review Workshop Notes		4 hrs	
86	3.3.2 Develop Definitions		1.5 days	85
87	3.3.3 Refine Architecture Model Diagrams		1 day?	85
95	3.3.4 Develop Standard Text	Quick Start Glossary Concepts	1.5 days	85
96	3.3.5 Quality Assurance Review		4 hrs	86,87,95
97	3.3.6 Publish Workshop Documentation		4 hrs	96
98	3.4 Workshop Review Meeting		1 day	84
99	3.4.1 Review Objectives and Agenda		1 hr	
100	3.4.2 Review Diagrams and Definitions		4 hrs	99
101	3.4.3 Resolve Open Issues		3 hrs	100
102	3.5 Prepare Implementation Models' matrices		1 day?	
103	3.5.1 Prepare Model Matrices		1 day?	
114	4 Enterprise Model Analysis - Tasks	Quick Start Checklist: Enterprise Model Analysis	14.63 days?	63
144	5 Review and Verification Tasks	Quick Start Checklist: Review and Verification	1 day	114
160	6 Analysis Transition Tasks	Quick Start Checklist: Analysis Transition Tasks	1 day	144

The detail of Enterprise Model Analysis:

File	Task	Resource	Project	View	Format				

	Task Name	Hyperlink	Duration	Predecessors
0	Quick Start Enterprise Architecture Plan	Visit the EACOE web site	54.38 days?	
1	1 Project Preparation	Quick Start Checklist: Project Preparation	13.75 days?	
44	2 Systems Inventory	Quick Start Checklist: Systems Inventory	13 days	1
63	3 Enterprise Modeling Tasks	Quick Start Checklist: Enterprise Modeling	11 days?	44
114	4 Enterprise Model Analysis - Tasks	Quick Start Checklist: Enterprise Model Analysis	14.63 days?	63
115	4.1 Develop Implementation Models		6.63 days?	
116	4.1.1 Present Implementation Modeling Education		1 hr	
117	4.1.2 Develop Initialized Implementation Model Matrices		6.13 days?	116
118	4.1.2.1 Required		2.13 days?	
119	4.1.2.1.1 Develop Processes Relate to Goals	Quick Start Implementation Model -Processes Relate to Goals	3 hrs	
120	4.1.2.1.2 Develop Processes Relate to Materials	Quick Start Implementation Model -Processes Relate to Materials	3 hrs	119
121	4.1.2.1.3 Develop Processes Relate to Systems	Quick Start Implementation Model -Processes Relate to Systems	3 hrs	120
122	4.1.2.1.4 Develop Processes Relate to Roles	Quick Start Implementation Model -Processes Relate to Roles	1 day?	121
123	4.1.2.2 Useful though optional/ Later		4 days?	122
124	4.1.2.2.1 Develop Processes Relate to Business Events	Quick Start Implementation Model -Processes Relate to Events	1 day?	
125	4.1.2.2.2 Develop Roles Relate to Business Events	Quick Start Implementation Model -Roles Relate to Events	1 day?	124
126	4.1.2.2.3 Develop Roles Relate to Locations	Quick Start Implementation Model -Roles Relate to Locations	1 day?	125
127	4.1.2.2.4 Develop Locations Relate to Systems	Quick Start Implementation Model -Locations Relate to Systems	1 day?	126
128	4.1.3 Review and Verify Implementation Model Matrices		3 hrs	127
129	4.2 Develop Initiative Boundaries	EACOE Quick Start -Developing Initiatives -Diagram	2 days	115
130	4.2.1 Perform Initial Affinity Analysis	EACOE Quick Start -Developing Initiatives	4 hrs	
131	4.2.2 Adjust Affinity Parameters		4 hrs	130
132	4.2.3 Refine Initiative Boundaries		4 hrs	131
133	4.2.4 Rank Initiatives		4 hrs	132
134	4.3 Initial Project Documentation		1 day	129
135	4.3.1 Develop Initial Project Documentation		1 day	
136	4.4 Conduct Initiative Ranking Review		2 days	134
137	4.4.1 Distribute Draft Executive Summary		1 hr	
138	4.4.2 Conduct 1 on 1 Executive Briefings		1.5 days	137
139	4.4.3 Conduct Executive Ranking Review Meeting		3 hrs	138
140	4.5 Produce Final Documentation		3 days	136
141	4.5.1 Produce Executive Summary		1 day	
142	4.5.2 Produce Initiative Descriptions		1 day	141
143	4.5.3 Produce Overall Enterprise Model	Quick Start Business on a Page Diagram	1 day	142
144	5 Review and Verification Tasks	Quick Start Checklist: Review and Verification	1 day	114
160	6 Analysis Transition Tasks	Quick Start Checklist: Analysis Transition Tasks	1 day	144

The detail of Review and Verification:

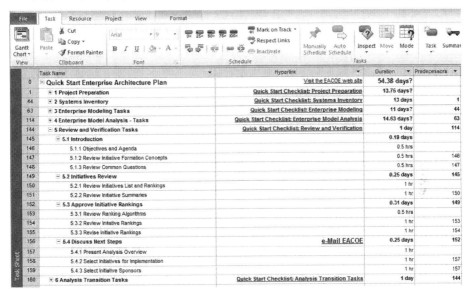

	Task Name	Hyperlink	Duration	Predecessors
0	Quick Start Enterprise Architecture Plan	Visit the EACOE web site	54.38 days?	
1	1 Project Preparation	Quick Start Checklist: Project Preparation	13.75 days?	
44	2 Systems Inventory	Quick Start Checklist: Systems Inventory	13 days	1
63	3 Enterprise Modeling Tasks	Quick Start Checklist: Enterprise Modeling	11 days?	44
114	4 Enterprise Model Analysis - Tasks	Quick Start Checklist: Enterprise Model Analysis	14.63 days?	63
144	5 Review and Verification Tasks	Quick Start Checklist: Review and Verification	1 day	114
145	5.1 Introduction		0.19 days	
146	5.1.1 Objectives and Agenda		0.5 hrs	
147	5.1.2 Review Initiative Formation Concepts		0.5 hrs	146
148	5.1.3 Review Common Questions		0.5 hrs	147
149	5.2 Initiatives Review		0.25 days	145
150	5.2.1 Review Initiatives List and Rankings		1 hr	
151	5.2.2 Review Initiative Summaries		1 hr	150
152	5.3 Approve Initiative Rankings		0.31 days	149
153	5.3.1 Review Ranking Algorithms		0.5 hrs	
154	5.3.2 Review Initiative Rankings		1 hr	153
155	5.3.3 Revise Initiative Rankings		1 hr	154
156	5.4 Discuss Next Steps	e-Mail EACOE	0.25 days	152
157	5.4.1 Present Analysis Overview		1 hr	
158	5.4.2 Select Initiatives for Implementation		1 hr	157
159	5.4.3 Select Initiative Sponsors		1 hr	157
160	6 Analysis Transition Tasks	Quick Start Checklist: Analysis Transition Tasks	1 day	144

The detail of Analysis Transition:

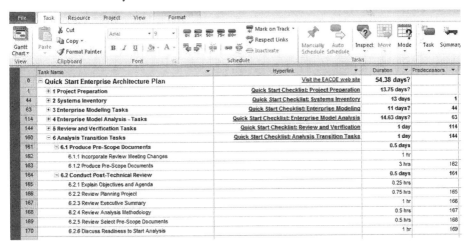

	Task Name	Hyperlink	Duration	Predecessors
0	Quick Start Enterprise Architecture Plan	Visit the EACOE web site	54.38 days?	
1	1 Project Preparation	Quick Start Checklist: Project Preparation	13.75 days?	
44	2 Systems Inventory	Quick Start Checklist: Systems Inventory	13 days	1
63	3 Enterprise Modeling Tasks	Quick Start Checklist: Enterprise Modeling	11 days?	44
114	4 Enterprise Model Analysis - Tasks	Quick Start Checklist: Enterprise Model Analysis	14.63 days?	63
144	5 Review and Verification Tasks	Quick Start Checklist: Review and Verification	1 day	114
160	6 Analysis Transition Tasks	Quick Start Checklist: Analysis Transition Tasks	1 day	144
161	6.1 Produce Pre-Scope Documents		0.5 days	
162	6.1.1 Incorporate Review Meeting Changes		1 hr	
163	6.1.2 Produce Pre-Scope Documents		3 hrs	162
164	6.2 Conduct Post-Technical Review		0.5 days	161
165	6.2.1 Explain Objectives and Agenda		0.25 hrs	
166	6.2.2 Review Planning Project		0.75 hrs	165
167	6.2.3 Review Executive Summary		1 hr	166
168	6.2.4 Review Analysis Methodology		0.5 hrs	167
169	6.2.5 Review Select Pre-Scope Documents		0.5 hrs	168
170	6.2.6 Discuss Readiness to Start Analysis		1 hr	169

EXAMPLE OF SKY HIGH GLIDERS PROCESS RELATIONSHIPS IMPLEMENTATION MODEL

This section includes examples of the Sky High Gliders Process descriptions as well as related Goals, Materials, Roles, and systems names. The information can also be found on the Implementation Models created in the enterprise model analysis phase. In this short example, definitions for most of the Enterprise Architecture artifacts are not included. In practice, a definition of each artifact is absolutely imperative and must not be skipped. Without solid definitions for all of the artifacts, considerable confusion exists in most organizations.

Notice how some Processes' relationships are very involved while others appear quite weak; watch for these keys as you assess complexity and candidates for removal or further analysis.

0 Sky High Gliders Processes

Sky High Gliders Processes is concerned with performing the activities required to achieve the enterprise's mission, goals, and objectives.

1 Manage Equipment

Manage Equipment is concerned with overseeing all equipment, including planning, acquiring, maintaining, and disposing of tangible goods directly involved with delivering our service to customers.

1.1 Plan Equipment Needs

Plan Equipment Needs involves forecasting and recommending changes to the quantity and type of equipment owned by Sky High Gliders.

Requires Materials	Supports Goals	Involves Roles	Mechanized by System
1.1 Wings	1.2 Open Kauai Operations	02 General Manager	
1.2 Harnesses	1.4 Expand Adventures by 50%		
1.3 Parachutes	1.5 Return Fair Profit		
1.4 Instruments		07 Marketing & Promotions	
1.5 Helmets	2.5 Expand Flying Tours		
1.6 Maintenance			
	3.1 Increase Glider Usage by 25%		
3.1 Locations			
3.5 Forecasts			
6.2 Capital			
6.4 Budgets			

1.2 Acquire Equipment

Acquire Equipment involves identifying equipment acquisition needs, ordering equipment from qualified suppliers, and accepting equipment in fulfillment of those orders.

Requires Materials	Supports Goals	Involves Roles	Mechanized by System
1.1 Wings	1.2 Open Kauai Operations	06 Maintenance	07 Maintenance Scheduling
1.2 Harnesses	1.4 Expand Adventures by 50%		
1.3 Parachutes			
1.4 Instruments	2.5 Expand Flying Tours		
1.5 Helmets			
1.6 Maintenance	3.1 Increase Glider Usage by 25%		
	3.3 Decrease Equipment Failures		
3.1 Locations			
6.1 Accounts			
6.2 Capital			
6.4 Budgets			
6.5 Policies			

1.3 Maintain Equipment

Maintain Equipment involves keeping equipment in peak operating condition.

Requires Materials	Supports Goals	Involves Roles	Mechanized by System
1.1 Wings	2.1 Achieve 40% Repeat Business	06 Maintenance	06 Maintenance Reporting
1.2 Harnesses			
1.3 Parachutes	3.3 Decrease Equipment Failures		07 Maintenance Scheduling
1.4 Instruments			
1.5 Helmets			
1.6 Maintenance			
3.1 Locations			
4.1 Package data			
6.1 Accounts			
6.2 Capital			
6.3 Risks			
6.4 Budgets			
6.5 Policies			

1.4 Retire Equipment

Retire Equipment involves disposing of equipment that is no longer needed in the most cost-effective manner.

Requires Materials	Supports Goals	Involves Roles	Mechanized by System
1.1 Wings	3.1 Increase Glider Usage by 25%	06 Maintenance	07 Maintenance Scheduling
1.2 Harnesses	3.3 Decrease Equipment Failures		
1.3 Parachutes			
1.4 Instruments			
1.5 Helmets			
1.6 Maintenance			
4.1 Package Data			
6.1 Accounts			
6.2 Capital			
6.3 Risks			
6.4 Budgets			
6.5 Policies			

2 Sell Lessons

Sell Lessons is concerned with completing sales of lessons, including identifying and satisfying the requirements of prospective students, qualifying them, and accepting lesson requests.

2.1 Receive Customer Leads

Receive Customer Leads involves identifying prospective customers and their lesson desires.

Requires Materials	Supports Goals	Involves Roles	Mechanized by System
2.1 Customer Data	1.3 Increase Promotions by 40%	08 Sales	03 Customer Evaluation Collection
2.2 Preferences	1.4 Expand Adventures by 50%		
3.3 Agents	3.1 Increase Glider Usage by 25%		

2.2 Propose Lessons

Propose Lessons involves providing lesson packages matching the needs of prospective customers.

Requires Materials	Supports Goals	Involves Roles	Mechanized by System
2.1 Customer Data 2.2 Preferences 3.3 Agents 4.1 Package Data 4.3 Package Types	1.2 Open Kauai Operations 1.4 Expand Adventures by 50% 2.1 Achieve 40% Repeat Business 2.2 Increase Pilot Certification Flexibility 3.1 Increase Glider Usage by 25%	07 Marketing & Promotions 08 Sales	03 Customer Evaluation Collection

2.3 Qualify Pilots

Qualify Pilots involves validating the skills of prospective previously rated pilots.

Requires Materials	Supports Goals	Involves Roles	Mechanized by System
2.1 Customer Data 2.2 Preferences 4.1 Package Data 4.2 Sales 4.3 Package Types 6.5 Policies	1.4 Expand Adventures by 50% 2.4 Achieve Zero Lesson Complaints 3.3 Decrease Equipment Failures 3.4 Prequalify All Customers	08 Sales	

2.4 Book Students

Book Students involves confirming a customer's lesson package purchase and scheduling required equipment and personnel.

Requires Materials	Supports Goals	Involves Roles	Mechanized by System
1.1 Wings	3.1 Increase Glider Usage by 25%	01 Lesson Operations	03 Customer Evaluation Collection
1.2 Harnesses			
1.3 Parachutes			
1.4 Instruments		03 Finance & Administration	
1.5 Helmets			
		04 Human Resources	
2.1 Customer Data			
3.3 Agents		08 Sales	
4.1 Package Data		09 Certification Operations	
4.2 Sales			
4.3 Package Types			
5.3 Skills			
6.1 Accounts			

3 Develop Markets

Develop Markets is concerned with expanding the number of prospective customers by managing locations, conducting promotions, managing agent accounts, and developing market forecasts.

3.1 Manage Locations

Manage Locations involves planning, acquiring, and maintaining base locations.

Requires Materials	Supports Goals	Involves Roles	Mechanized by System
2.2 Preferences	1.1 Double Number of Instructors 1.2 Open Kauai Operations	02 General Manager	01 Agent Reward Compensation
3.1 Locations 3.5 Forecasts	2.1 Achieve 40% Repeat Business 2.2 Increase Pilot Certification Flexibility	03 Finance & Administration	
6.1 Accounts 6.2 Capital 6.3 Risks 6.4 Budgets	2.3 Publish Handbooks in 2009	07 Marketing & Promotions	

3.2 Conduct Promotions

Conduct Promotions involves enhancing and expanding the market's knowledge of and desire for Sky High Gliders.

Requires Materials	Supports Goals	Involves Roles	Mechanized by System
1.1 Wings	1.1 Double Number of Instructors	07 Marketing & Promotions	
1.2 Harnesses	1.2 Open Kauai Operations		
1.3 Parachutes	1.3 Increase Promotions by 40%		
1.4 Instruments			
1.5 Helmets	2.1 Achieve 40% Repeat Business		
3.1 Locations			
3.2 Promotions	3.1 Increase Glider Usage by 25%		
3.3 Agents			
3.5 Forecasts			
4.2 Sales			
4.3 Package Types			
6.1 Accounts			
6.4 Budgets			

3.3 Manage Agent Accounts

Manage Agent Accounts involves enhancing the effectiveness of travel agents as a distribution channel for our adventures.

Requires Materials	Supports Goals	Involves Roles	Mechanized by System
2.1 Customer Data	1.1 Double Number of Instructors	07 Marketing & Promotions	
	1.2 Open Kauai Operations		
3.2 Promotions			
3.3 Agents	2.1 Achieve 40% Repeat Business		
4.2 Sales	3.1 Increase Glider Usage by 25%		
6.1 Accounts			
6.4 Budgets			

3.4 Develop Market Forecasts

Develop Market Forecasts involves assessing future market needs and conditions.

Requires Materials	Supports Goals	Involves Roles	Mechanized by System
1.1 Wings	1.2 Open Kauai Operations	07 Marketing & Promotions	
1.2 Harnesses			
1.3 Parachutes	2.1 Achieve 40% Repeat Business		
1.4 Instruments	2.5 Expand Flying Tours		
1.5 Helmets			
2.1 Customer Data			
2.2 Preferences			
3.1 Locations			
3.4 Competitors			
3.5 Forecasts			
4.2 Sales			
4.3 Package Types			

4 Develop Adventures

Develop Adventures is concerned with extending the range of adventures offered and includes defining and releasing new adventure offerings and enhancing current adventure offerings.

4.1 Analyze Customer Preferences

Analyze Customer Preferences involves assessing customer preference information.

Requires Materials	Supports Goals	Involves Roles	Mechanized by System
2.2 Preferences 4.2 Sales	1.2 Open Kauai Operations 1.5 Return Fair Profit 2.1 Achieve 40% Repeat Business 2.2 Increase Pilot Certification Flexibility 2.3 Publish Handbooks in 2009 2.5 Expand Flying Tours 3.5 Institute Education Requirements		02 Customer Scheduling

4.2 Receive Market Forecasts

Receive Market Forecasts involves collecting market forecast information.

Requires Materials	Supports Goals	Involves Roles	Mechanized by System
3.5 Forecasts	1.5 Return Fair Profit 2.2 Increase Pilot Certification Flexibility		

4.3 Design Adventures

Design Adventures involves creating the definition and structure of new offerings, such as where the adventure is located, what adventure options are available, whether any promotions will be required for the new adventure, and the pricing of each adventure.

Requires Materials	Supports Goals	Involves Roles	Mechanized by System
1.1 Wings 1.2 Harnesses 1.3 Parachutes 1.4 Instruments 1.5 Helmets	1.2 Open Kauai Operations 1.5 Return Fair Profit 2.1 Achieve 40% Repeat Business 2.2 Increase Pilot Certification Flexibility 2.5 Expand Flying Tours	01 Lesson Operations 02 General Manager 07 Marketing & Promotions	03 Customer Evaluation Collection

2.2 Preferences	3.5 Institute Education Requirements	08 Sales	
3.1 Locations		09 Certification Operations	
3.4 Competitors			
3.5 Forecasts			
4.1 Package Data			
4.3 Package Types			

4.4 Measure Adventure Satisfaction

Measure Adventure Satisfaction involves analyzing customer evaluations and determining their relative satisfaction over time.

Requires Materials	Supports Goals	Involves Roles	Mechanized by System
2.1 Customer Data 4.1 Package Data	2.1 Achieve 40% Repeat Business 2.2 Increase Pilot Certification Flexibility 2.5 Expand Flying Tours		

4.5 Improve Adventures

Improve Adventures involves gathering and analyzing the information required to enhance glider adventure definitions based on customer evaluations.

Requires Materials	Supports Goals	Involves Roles	Mechanized by System
1.1 Wings	2.1 Achieve 40% Repeat Business		03 Customer Evaluation Collection
1.2 Harnesses	2.2 Increase Pilot Certification Flexibility		
1.3 Parachutes			
1.4 Instruments			
1.5 Helmets			
2.2 Preferences			
3.1 Locations			
3.4 Competitors			
3.5 Forecasts			
4.1 Package Data			
4.3 Package Types			

5 Conduct Certifications

Conduct Certifications is concerned with performing our pilot certification program, including preparing lesson plans, outfitting students, and processing departures and certifications.

5.1 Prepare Lesson Plans

Prepare Lesson Plans involves ensuring that the lesson plans for all students choosing to receive pilot certification are created and approved by the Senior Instructor.

Requires Materials	Supports Goals	Involves Roles	Mechanized by System
1.1 Wings	2.1 Achieve 40% Repeat Business	01 Lesson Operations	02 Customer Scheduling
1.2 Harnesses	2.4 Achieve Zero Lesson Complaints		
1.3 Parachutes		09 Certification Operations	
1.4 Instruments	3.3 Decrease Equipment Failures		
1.5 Helmets			
1.6 Maintenance			
2.2 Preferences			
4.1 Package Data			
4.2 Sales			

5.2 Outfit Students

Outfit Students involves gathering all equipment and ensuring that it fits properly before certification begins.

Requires Materials	Supports Goals	Involves Roles	Mechanized by System
1.1 Wings 1.2 Harnesses 1.3 Parachutes 1.4 Instruments 1.5 Helmets	2.1 Achieve 40% Repeat Business 2.4 Achieve Zero Lesson Complaints		02 Customer Scheduling

5.3 Process Departures

Process Departures involves orienting the customers to the particular glider configuration and optional equipment included in the glider package, briefing customers on local weather patterns, and handing out guidebooks and aviation charts.

Requires Materials	Supports Goals	Involves Roles	Mechanized by System
1.1 Wings 1.2 Harnesses 1.3 Parachutes 1.4 Instruments 1.5 Helmets 4.1 Package Data 4.2 Sales 5.1 Employees 6.1 Accounts	2.1 Achieve 40% Repeat Business 3.2 Develop Multi-Lesson Package		02 Customer Scheduling

5.4 Process Certification Completions

Process Certification Completions involves processing proficiency and certification paperwork, inspecting and cleaning equipment, and seeking customer feedback on the certification process.

Requires Materials	Supports Goals	Involves Roles	Mechanized by System
1.1 Wings	2.1 Achieve 40% Repeat Business	01 Lesson Operations	02 Customer Scheduling
1.2 Harnesses	2.4 Achieve Zero Lesson Complaints		
1.3 Parachutes			
1.4 Instruments		09 Certification Operations	03 Customer Evaluation Collection
1.5 Helmets	3.2 Develop Multi-Lesson Package		
1.6 Maintenance	3.3 Decrease Equipment Failures		
2.1 Customer Data			
4.1 Package Data			
5.1 Employees			
6.1 Accounts			

6 Manage Human Resources

Manage Human Resources is concerned with overseeing human resource needs, including planning, acquiring, supervising, developing, and terminating employees.

6.1 Develop Staffing Plans

Develop Staffing Plans involves assessing future requirements for employees based on manpower and skill requirements of the enterprise.

Requires Materials	Supports Goals	Involves Roles	Mechanized by System
3.1 Locations	1.1 Double Number of Instructors	02 General Manager	
3.5 Forecasts	1.2 Open Kauai Operations		
5.2 Positions	1.5 Return Fair Profit	03 Finance & Administration	
5.3 Skills	3.5 Institute Education Requirements	04 Human Resources	
5.4 Compensation			
6.4 Budgets		05 Information Technology	

6.2 Acquire Employees

Acquire Employees involves recruiting, offering, and accepting new employees.

Requires Materials	Supports Goals	Involves Roles	Mechanized by System
3.1 Locations	1.1 Double Number of Instructors	04 Human Resources	
	1.2 Open Kauai Operations		
5.1 Employees	1.3 Increase Promotions by 40%		
5.2 Positions	1.5 Return Fair Profit		
5.3 Skills			
5.4 Compensation	2.3 Publish Handbooks in 2009		
6.1 Accounts			
6.4 Budgets			

6.3 Assess Employee Performance

Assess Employee Performance involves assigning, controlling, and assessing performance of work performed by employees.

Requires Materials	Supports Goals	Involves Roles	Mechanized by System
5.1 Employees 5.2 Positions 5.3 Skills 5.4 Compensation	2.1 Achieve 40% Repeat Business	01 Lesson Operations 02 General Manager 03 Finance & Administration 04 Human Resources 05 Information Technology 06 Maintenance 07 Marketing & Promotions 08 Sales 09 Certification Operations	

6.4 Develop Education Programs

Develop Education Programs involves enhancing and expanding employee skills, including but not limited to preparation for the new glider services. We anticipate that these programs will become the foundation for the education glider services to be offered in the future.

Requires Materials	Supports Goals	Involves Roles	Mechanized by System
1.1 wings	1.1 double number of instructors	02 general manager	
1.2 harnesses	1.5 return fair profit		
1.3 parachutes		03 finance & administration	
1.4 instruments	2.1 achieve 40% repeat business		
1.5 helmets		04 human resources	
4.3 package types			
5.1 employees		05 information technology	
5.5 development		06 maintenance	
		07 marketing & promotions	
		08 sales	
		09 certification operations	

6.5 Train Employees

Train Employees involves identifying the training needs of individual employees, enrolling them into specific classes and conducting the training classes.

Requires Materials	Supports Goals	Involves Roles	Mechanized by System
1.1 Wings	1.1 Double Number of Instructors		
1.2 Harnesses	1.5 Return Fair Profit		
1.3 Parachutes			
1.4 Instruments	3.2 Develop Multi-Lesson Package		
1.5 Helmets			
5.1 Employees			
5.2 Positions			
5.3 Skills			
5.5 Development			

6.6 Terminate Employees

Terminate Employees involves removing the relationship between the enterprise and employee.

Requires Materials	Supports Goals	Involves Roles	Mechanized by System
3.1 Locations		02 General Manager	
3.5 Forecasts			
		04 Human Resources	
5.1 Employees			
5.2 Positions			
5.3 Skills			
6.1 Accounts			
6.4 Budgets			

7 Manage Finances

Manage Finances is concerned with acquiring, controlling, and reporting the fiscal requirements, including managing transactions, capital, and risks; developing budgets; monitoring policy compliance; and providing financial information.

7.1 Manage Transactions

Manage Transactions involves identifying, classifying, and controlling monetary transactions in accordance with generally accepted accounting principles.

Requires Materials	Supports Goals	Involves Roles	Mechanized by System
3.1 Locations	3.2 Develop Multi-Lesson Package	03 Finance & Administration	01 Agent Reward Compensation
3.5 Forecasts			
			02 Customer Scheduling
4.1 Package Data			
			04 Finance Reporting
6.1 Accounts			
6.5 Policies			
			05 General Ledger
			06 Maintenance Reporting

7.2 Manage Capital

Manage Capital involves acquiring and safeguarding the financial resources.

Requires Materials	Supports Goals	Involves Roles	Mechanized by System
1.1 Wings	1.1 Double Number of Instructors	03 Finance & Administration	04 Finance Reporting
1.2 Harnesses			
1.3 Parachutes	1.2 Open Kauai Operations		
1.4 Instruments			05 General Ledger
1.5 Helmets	2.5 Expand Flying Tours		
3.1 Locations			
6.1 Accounts			
6.2 Capital			
6.3 Risks			
6.4 Budgets			
6.5 Policies			

7.3 Manage Risks

Manage Risks involves controlling the variability of financial returns due to the risks inherent in our industry.

Requires Materials	Supports Goals	Involves Roles	Mechanized by System
1.1 Wings	3.3 Decrease Equipment Failures		
1.2 Harnesses	3.4 Prequalify All Customers		
1.3 Parachutes	3.5 Institute Education Requirements		
1.4 Instruments			
1.5 Helmets			
1.6 Maintenance			
3.5 Forecasts			
4.1 Package Data			
4.3 Package Types			
5.5 Development			
6.2 Capital			
6.3 Risks			
6.5 Policies			

7.4 Develop Budgets

Develop Budgets involves receiving budget constraints from the parent organization, allocating and controlling funding of individual organization units through time, and obtaining approval of Sky High Gliders's budget priorities from RAI.

Requires Materials	Supports Goals	Involves Roles	Mechanized by System
4.2 Sales	1.1 Double Number of Instructors	01 Lesson Operations	04 Finance Reporting
	1.2 Open Kauai Operations	02 General Manager	05 General Ledger
5.4 Compensation	1.3 Increase Promotions by 40%		
5.5 Development		03 Finance & Administration	
6.1 Accounts		04 Human Resources	
6.2 Capital			
6.3 Risks		05 Information Technology	
6.4 Budgets			
		06 Maintenance	
		07 Marketing & Promotions	
		08 Sales	
		09 Certification Operations	

7.5 Monitor Policy Compliance

Monitor Policy Compliance involves auditing conformance to the stated policies of the enterprise and making recommendations for changes to either the operational practices or corporate policies where appropriate.

Requires Materials	Supports Goals	Involves Roles	Mechanized by System
6.1 Accounts			
6.2 Capital			
6.3 Risks			
6.4 Budgets			
6.5 Policies			

7.6 Provide Financial Information

Provide Financial Information involves collecting, analyzing, formatting, and publishing financial results to internal and external organizations.

Requires Materials	Supports Goals	Involves Roles	Mechanized by System
4.2 Sales	1.1 Double Number of Instructors	02 General Manager	04 Finance Reporting
	1.2 Open Kauai Operations		
6.1 Accounts		03 Finance & Administration	05 General Ledger
6.4 Budgets	3.2 Develop Multi-Lesson Package		
6.5 Policies			
		05 Information Technology	

APPENDIX D:

ENTERPRISE ARCHITECTURE ROADMAPS

Your-Company

Moving Forward
(a very small and limited example!)

Produced to reflect Pinnacle Roadmaps as examples only
based on artificial information
for a mythical "Your-Company"

A Document of Analysis,
Logical Conclusions, and
Recommendations

Moving Your Enterprise Forward

prepared for
Your-Company

by

Pinnacle Business Group, Inc.
10895 Lakepointe Drive
Pinckney, MI 48169
(810) 231-0531

Summary of Efforts

Pinnacle Business Group, Inc. (Pinnacle) has worked closely with members of Your-Company's team since 1Q12. Together, we have progressively built and analyzed a foundational base model for understanding Your-Company's Corporate and technology activities.

Our initial efforts developed several models and perspectives of the Corporate and technology vision for a world-class organization, its Business Relationship initiatives, goals, and success metrics, and modeled a number of processes. As input to these efforts, Pinnacle extensively analyzed Your-Company's documents and online information, which we list in appendix A, "Your-Company Source Documents for Initial Efforts." We captured the results of these efforts in the documents listed in appendix B, "Pinnacle Documents."

Pinnacle began the detailed Corporate Phase-I effort to establish a strong, extensible model of Your-Company's business activities; inventory existing applications, their operational health, and their support of these business activities; analyze and improve the corporate processes; identify incumbent vendor coverage of business activities, deployment opportunities, cost allocation, and governance; develop initial Process Visualizations™ for a set of prioritized business processes spanning business client areas; and establish a Normative Language Glossary for consistent communication between business staff members and between business and technology staff members. Pinnacle continued these efforts by building on the earlier results, analyzing additional Your-Company documents, online information, and industry materials listed in appendix C, "Your-Company Source Documents." The results of this detailed corporate effort are listed in appendix D: Pinnacle Documents.

Pinnacle's continuing efforts conclude with this consolidated report of projects and Pinnacle Methodology-derived "Roadmaps" (Pinnacle Roadmaps), moving these efforts forward to guide the organization to its desired state five years from now in the most agile manner possible. Within this report, we include projects for formulating a model for the Business and for developing the Business Relationship Management success model. We track the relevant materials for this continued analysis in appendix E, "Your-Company Source Documents," and have generated the additional supporting documents listed in appendix F, "Pinnacle Documents."

Defining Pinnacle Roadmaps

Your-Company has a wide scope of exciting opportunities, and to successfully convey this large amount of information, we present the recommendations in subsets of focus areas. Pinnacle's experience guides us to form efforts around activities and not around administrative organization structures; therefore, we have developed multiple Pinnacle Roadmaps that will each suggest participation across Your-Company's staff.

Each Pinnacle Roadmap groups together related recommended efforts in order of priority. We refer to these recommended efforts as "projects" to simplify the presentation, though each may range from simple, low-resource actions to sets of interrelated, long-term endeavors. We include for each Pinnacle Roadmap visual tools: a summary table of the roadmap's projects and a risk mapping of the roadmap's projects. We consolidate these graphics into the Executive Summary that follows. Pinnacle supports its recommended projects with our assessment and observations that lead us to the conclusion defining the need. We group projects together if they arise from a single conclusion. Finally, in each project, we list a set of recommended steps or actions that may fast-start the effort.

Your-Company's Preference

Your-Company should review these recommendations with an eye toward refining the recommendations and their prioritization. Finally, Pinnacle asserts priorities for these recommended projects based on our best knowledge of the Your-Company vision and priorities.

Executive Summary

Your-Company seeks to improve its effectiveness, efficiency, and support of business clients. Pinnacle has analyzed extensive Your-Company business and technology documents, and, building on the results of our earlier efforts and realizations, suggests that Your-Company consider these recommendations moving forward:

Major Findings (EXAMPLES AND SAMPLES ONLY ACROSS VARIOUS DOMAINS!)

1. *Invest in Business Relationships:* Successful business relationships will require focus, guidance, and resources to succeed; Corporate management seeks to transition to the role of Business Relationship Managers. Business Relationship Managers will be in a key position to drive many of the recommended actions to success. The plans for achieving this Business Relationship Management transition are extensive, and call for significant commitment from Your-Company Business and technology management.

   See Roadmap 1: Business Relationship Management.

2. *Improve Data Security:* Many applications have no security systems or are missing information for the data security attributes, although most applications have an authentication system. A large number of applications have no data encryption method listed or the data are unknown or missing. Your-Company data could be at risk.

   See Roadmap 3: Data and System Integrity

3. *Consolidate Coordination of Cross Lines-of-Business Initiatives:* These Enterprise initiatives have complex interactions. The global and marketing focused initiatives have several veins of common dependencies and need to be carefully coordinated.

   See Roadmap 2: Cross Lines-of-Business

4. *Establish Consistent Methods for Financial Forecasting:* Your-Company presently has no standard method or guidelines for making financial forecasts. Your-Company should establish recommendations and guidelines for financial forecasting business rules, based on best practices.
See Roadmap 6: Financial IT Planning

5. *Automate Financial Planning Processes:* Your-Company should purchase or build a new budget, planning, and forecasting application to streamline financial forecasting and eliminate, or greatly reduce, the time-consuming use of spreadsheets.
See Roadmap 6: Financial IT Planning

6. *Complete Application Health Check Data:* Many common application attributes are not well known by the technology and business groups that use them, compromising the effectiveness of the Application Health Check. Your-Company can gain a great deal of operational and planning knowledge by completing these items in the Application Health Check.
See Roadmap 3: Data and System Integrity
   Roadmap 7: Enterprise Architecture

7. *Calculate Reliability:* Reliability has not been calculated for most applications in the Application Health Check, preventing an assessment of critical business process stability.
See Roadmap 3: Data and System Integrity

8. *Improve Application Quality:* One of the Your-Company Enterprise goals is to achieve outstanding customer satisfaction. In view of this goal, too many applications are rated "low" or "medium."
See Roadmap 4: Application Quality

9. *Improve Application Documentation:* Application documentation is inadequate. Furthermore, application documentation information resides separately from other attributes, hindering comparison to other application attributes.
See Roadmap 3: Data and System Integrity

10. ***Assist Businesses to Visualize Consistent Process Improvements:***
Each area identifies processes that need to be improved. Each
Corporate Business area notes several processes it professes to
improve in this next year (FYxx); the processes need to be carefully
understood to reengineer them to meet the Your-Company vision
and goals.
See Roadmap 8: Process Visualization™

11. ***Update Licensed Technologies to Current Releases:*** Many
technologies are several releases back-level. Many supporting
applications, databases, and other technologies are not recent with
respect to current levels of release. Your-Company may be exposed
to service gaps and additional upgrade costs.
See Roadmap 7: Enterprise Architecture

12. ***Assess Masked Technology Impacts:*** Significant cumulative
technology impact may be implicated; many businesses note
significant initiatives and projects that discuss technology
involvement that is not clearly identified. Business Relationship
Managers' review can identify most such expectations early to avoid
resource crisis beyond the planning cycle.
See Roadmap 1: Business Relationship Management, page 249,
Roadmap 2: Cross Lines-of-Business
Roadmap 4: Application Quality
Roadmap 5: Incumbent Vendor Function Realization, and
Roadmap 9: CIO Governance and Coordination

Pinnacle recommends 125 project actions distributed across ten (10)
balanced *Pinnacle Roadmaps:*

1. *Business Relationship Management*

   The Business Relationship Management Roadmap gathers
   recommended projects that deal with improving and expanding
   the collaboration with the business areas to have the role of
   trusted advisors and partners.

These projects will:

> Formalize Business Executive communications;
>
> Build Business Relationship Managers' liaison skills;
>
> Improve knowledge of client business drivers;
>
> Evolve Technology Services from project-based to full-service relationships;
>
> Model and maintain an understanding of evolving business goals;
>
> Proactively investigate business initiatives for guidance; and
>
> Assess business areas' plans to discover probable IT impacts not yet recognized, clearly documented, or funded by the business.

2. *Cross Lines-of-Business*

This Cross Lines-of-Business Roadmap gathers cross-department and business segment concerns and projects that deal less with specific business areas and more with broad-based support solutions, including cross-segment marketing and cosponsored events. This Roadmap deals with issues that impact cross-segment areas of service and support delivery.

These projects will:

> Verify cross-segment application capabilities and utilization;
>
> Build and extend the infrastructures for customer data integration and Consumer Relationship Management;
>
> Develop cross Lines-of-Business client data, enabling coordinated campaigns to benefit all business unit marketing goals;
>
> Expand cobranded business capabilities;
>
> Implement measures to track growth, standards, and demand;
>
> Improve and replace international documentation management systems;
>
> Improve large file handling and sharing across all business units;

Analyze cross-business unit complex applications for extracting valued capabilities as widely reusable components;

Verify that business expectations of existing applications are within the capabilities of the application's design; and

Assess cross-segment plans to discover probable impacts not yet recognized, clearly documented, or funded by the business.

3. *Application Quality*

The Application Quality Roadmap gathers projects that deal with improving business clients' satisfaction with technologies in use. The focus in this Roadmap is on improved quality and performance of the applications from business and operational perspectives.

These projects will:

Identify weaknesses and implement quality improvements in business satisfaction, flexibility, technical support, and vision enablement;

Measure and track application reliability;

Document key application support information;

Improve Management Reporting quality; and

Improve Anti-Piracy capabilities.

4. *Financial Planning*

The Financial Planning Roadmap gathers recommended projects that will make Your-Company budgeting and financial forecasting processes more efficient, accurate, and timely by moving away from the existing spreadsheet-based process to a new software tool for managing data input, consolidation, approval, and reporting.

These projects will:

Select and standardize key financial variables needed to run the business;

Establish recommendations and guidelines for financial forecasting business rules based on best practices; and

Implement a new financial planning process and software tool.

5. *Enterprise Architecture*

The Enterprise Architecture (EA) Roadmap gathers projects that establish architecture and guidance for operations and development, projects that maximize assets' value by improving reuse and reducing complexity, and projects that keep relevant the foundational EA models that Your-Company will need to maintain a world-class organization.

These projects will:

Develop a cross Line-of-Business Management architecture;

Develop a continuing application health check process;

Select preferred development technologies;

Establish a data platform architecture;

Pursue highly reusable assets, one-process to one-implementation;

Investigate opportunities to extract highly reusable assets from bundled applications;

Maintain and keep relevant the Your-Company EA models; and

Maintain and keep relevant the Your-Company Glossary of a Normative Language.

6. *Process Visualization*™

The Process Visualization Roadmap gathers business-process-oriented projects together. This is a broad scope that deals with nearly all aspects of the Your-Company business activities.

These projects will:

> Visualize and document key business processes and their requirements;
>
> Evaluate business processes for common needs;
>
> Establish business process change governance;
>
> Expand upon earlier business process visualizations;
>
> Improve Area 1 processes;
>
> Improve Area 2 processes;
>
> Improve Managerial Reporting processes;
>
> Improve Area 4 Management processes;
>
> Improve Area 5 processes;
>
> Improve Area 6 and Area 6A processes;
>
> Improve Customer Relationship Management processes; and
>
> Improve Area 7 processes.

7. **CIO Governance and Coordination**

The CIO Governance and Coordination Roadmap gathers cross-concern interests and projects that deal with some specific business areas. This broad-scope Roadmap deals with cross-concern areas of governance, application value, application and technology licensing, and assessing the impact of several business-area-specific interests.

These projects will:

> Improve governance and incumbent vendor change management;
>
> Proactively seek to confirm and verify business expectations;

Assess applications' contemporary value;

Verify and track corporate and enterprise licensing obligations; and

Assess with Business Relationship Management their business areas' plans to discover probable impacts not yet recognized, clearly documented, or funded by the business.

Executive Summary: Roadmap Summary Tables

Roadmap 1: Business Relationship Management

Roadmap Project Titles	Analysis	Conclusion	Priority	Desired End State
1.1 Formalize Executive Communications	Business and technology expectations need to be aligned.	Ensure demand and expectations are reasonable within budgets and priorities	Critical	Positive, collaborative business Executive relationships
1.1.1 Enhance Communications skills				
1.1.2 Enhance Relationship skills				
1.1.3 Enhance Enterprise Architecture skills				
1.1.4 Enhance Personnel skills				
1.1.5 Enhance Planning skills				
1.1.6 Enhance Guidance skills				
1.2 Understand CRM business drivers	Global market and technology influences change often and need to be continuously evaluated and understood.	Understand direct market influence on needs	Critical	Effective and proactive support for global marketing
1.3 Evolve to full-service relationship				

1.4 Understand Legal business drivers 1.5 Assess Legal projects impact	Legal Corporate requirements have complex e-document projects. They should aim to reduce handling of physical files and add "discovery" search	Understand list of processes that cross corporate groups and segments	Critical	Coordinated and balanced inter-dependent projects
1.6 Understand HR (Human Resource) business drivers 1.7 Assess HR projects impact	HR applications are dispersed and some processes are highly manual	Increased HR complexity requires greater understanding of the degree of automation possible	Important	Proactive plans to automate complex processes
1.8 Model business goals 1.9 Proactively investigate Business initiatives	Project requests have queued up beyond the resources of the technology organization	Understand the priorities and business direction of clients	Important	Clear, up-to-date view of business direction
1.10 Assess Sourcing and Procurement projects impact	Sourcing and Procurement initiatives may have technology impact	Determine if Sourcing and Procurement will require greater technology involvement	Becomes Important	Proactive technology Providing Timely Solutions

Executive Summary: Roadmap Risk Mappings

Pinnacle rated the projects according to the business risk if Your-Company takes no action. The Proprietary risk assessment method considered two factors: the probability that an issue will occur and the severity of the impact on Your-Company should it occur. Again, these are estimates that Your-Company should refine as needed. Pinnacle Business Group, Inc. has developed this rating system to assist in visually understanding and gauging large portfolios of projects.

We rated the *probability* that an issue will occur on a five-level scale:
- Improbable   Less than 1% chance[1]
- Remote   1% up to 5%
- Occasional   5% up to 10%
- Probable   10% up to 25%
- Frequent   25%+

We rated the *severity* of the impact on Your-Company should the issue occur on a four-level scale:

Metric[2] Clients	TIME Metric	COST Metric	Quality Perception to Clients
Negligible	Minutes	Dollars	Nuisance
Marginal	Hours	$1,000s (Ks)	Inconvenient
Critical	Many hours	$10Ks	Upset Clients looking for alternates
Catastrophic	Days	$100Ks	Lost Client business, litigation

The name of each project appears in the box corresponding to the project's probability and impact assessments. Projects in boxes toward the upper right corner of the grid should be addressed first, because the probability of an issue occurring is the highest and the business impact on Your-Company is the most severe if no action is taken. Projects toward the lower left of the grid are less urgent.

---

1   Actual percentage thresholds here are arbitrary; Your-Company should set these as it determines what thresholds are most representative of its business risk.

2   Pinnacle provides these example perspectives of how an impact might be perceived through differing pain-points; Your-Company should define its impact metrics to reflect the conditions that most represent its critical success factors.

Roadmap 1: Business Relationship Management –Project Risk

Severity of Impact	Improbable	Remote	Occasional	Probable	Frequent
Catastrophic					
Critical				1.4 Understand Legal business drivers	1.1 Formalize Executive Communications 1.2 Understand CRM business drivers 1.3 Evolve to full-service relationship
Marginal			1.8 Model Business Goals	1.9 Proactively Investigate Business Initiatives 1.6 Understand HR business drivers	
Negligible		1.5 Assess Legal projects impact 1.7 Assess HR projects impact 1.10 Assess Sourcing and Procurement projects impact			

Probability that an issue occurs
If Projects not pursued

Severity of Impact

Roadmap 1: Business Relationship Management

The Business Relationship Management Roadmap gathers recommended projects that deal with improving and expanding the collaboration with the business areas to become trusted advisors and partners.

We present recommended project titles in **bold** and numbered (**1.i.i**).

1.1 Formalize Executive Communications

Evolve the current role of Business Relationship Managers who are responsible for their key client business areas' expectations, funding, and satisfaction. The Business Relationship Manager will establish personal business communications with each client business executive and prepare both the executive and the Business Relationship Manager to work together in setting a course of action.

> Our observations found a mismatch of expectations between technology and its business clients, which had resulted in business expecting more projects than can be performed with the available resources and funding. It is important that business decision makers have a direct voice to ensure that their key objectives will be met without confusion or delay. We believe that positive, collaborative relationships with their business clients is required to ensure that demand and expectations are reasonable and within the budgets and priorities of the Your-Company enterprise.

We suggest these steps as one approach to address this issue:
1. Establish introductory expectations with each executive area
2. Discuss plans with executives to build relationships
3. Confer on suggested business-specific awareness to improve
4. Share understandings of resource commitments, limitations, and expectations
5. Plan and Prepare follow-up meetings
   a. Set a concise agenda: respect valuable executive time
   b. Keep documents and executive tasks to the minimum

1.1.1 Develop Business Relationship Manager Communications Skills

Develop the Business Relationship Managers' business and interpersonal communications skills to enhance the success of their critical role.

We suggest these initial steps:
1. Build communication plans
2. Craft communications messages
3. Improve interviewing skills

1.1.2 Develop Business Relationship Management Relationship Skills

Develop the Business Relationship Managers' relationship skills to help them establish long-term working partnerships.

We suggest these initial steps:
1. Improve Networking Skills
2. Improve Executive Relationship Building Skills

1.1.3 Develop Business Relationship Manager Enterprise Architecture Skills

Develop the Business Relationship Managers' Enterprise Architecture skills to ensure that they can guide business requests to align with goals and meet the Governance vision.

We suggest these initial steps:
1. Educate on Enterprise Architecture Concepts
2. Provide training on Business Process Engineering
3. Provide training on creating Business Models
4. Provide training on maintaining Systems and Assets inventories
5. Provide training on current Project Management best practices

1.1.4 Develop Business Relationship Manager Personnel Skills

Develop the Business Relationship Managers' personnel management skills to ensure they can quickly address issues and guide their teams to meet their project milestones.

We suggest these initial steps:
1. Develop performance measurement concepts
2. Understand escalation processes
3. Pursue activity-based costing concepts
4. Focus on client satisfaction
5. Understand use of basic statistics
6. Clarify organizational responsibilities

1.1.5 Develop Business Relationship Manager Strategic Planning Skills

Develop the Business Relationship Managers' strategic planning skills to ensure that they clearly understand and can convey the technology vision and obstacles that may conflict with desired business goals.

We suggest these initial steps:
1. Develop strategy and planning processes
2. Provide training on strategic thinking
3. Provide mentoring on preparing strategic initiatives
4. Provide training on change management

1.1.6 Develop Business Relationship Manager Guidance Skills

Develop the Business Relationship Managers' guidance skills to enable them to provide insightful business alternatives in trends and capabilities.

We suggest these initial steps:
1. Perform Business Industry Insight Analysis
2. Perform Technology Industry Insight Analysis
3. Enhance Presentation Skills
4. Enhance Organization Skills

1.2 Understand Customer Relationship Management Business Drivers

Business Relationship Managers need to gain and maintain an understanding of the current and trending business drivers that form the substantial requirements base for extending global Customer Data Integration (CDI) and Consumer Relationship Marketing (CRM) to Cooperatively Optimized

Relationships (COR).

Your Company's US model of shared customer data is successful, and is the basis for extensive work initiatives. The cross segment and international demands on these next generation data engines will be driven by new business market opportunity and technology. These are moving targets, so it is important to stay apprised of the current trends.

We conclude that while Corporate will be expected to deliver to CRM and other management a flexible and powerful data engine, the direct market influence on these capabilities is still not clearly documented.

We suggest these initial steps as one approach to address this issue:

1. Identify CRM strengths, dependencies, limitations, and issues
2. Identify emerging market trends in technology marketing
3. Train staff on CRM current state, industry direction, and potential value
4. Identify market-specific examples of technology dependence
5. Collaborate on processes for recommending new efforts
6. Develop a plan to move toward Cooperatively Optimized Relationships (COR).

1.3 Evolve to full-service relationships

Business Relationship Managers needs to transform their support model to become a partner to their business clients, serving as an expert liaison. They will guide the evolution of the business to provide intuitive tools and interfaces and the full-service ideas of inception-to-live capability for guidance, drawing out for the business their best expectations.

The Marketing initiatives are complex, and the demand is clear. Customer Relationship Management will also be pressed to deal with numerous technology changes and training. The greater the support they receive from the services areas, the less frustrated they will be and the fewer shortcuts they will take.

We conclude that with several years of business challenges ahead, Your-Company corporate businesses will need to focus on their top skills and less on their dependence on services; the services should become a "given" solid resource with proactive Business Relationship Management and reliable, easy-to-use business functions.

We suggest these initial steps as one approach to address this issue:

1. Identify key points in the development life cycle
   a. Formulate a business "evolutionary development" mentality
2. Train staff and Customer Relationship Management interface staff on the Business Relationship Management advisor approach
3. Develop Subject Matter Experts for Customer Relationship Management.

Frequently Asked Questions

Question: **Can I buy a generic Enterprise Architecture?**

Answer: There is no such thing as an Enterprise Architecture (or model, or series of models) that will fit any organization. You might be able to leverage components from an internal prior effort, but you should review anything like that against your organization's Goals, Processes, and Materials requirements *after* you develop your models. You need to define your enterprise's own DNA first. We don't recommend the practice of using "reference" models or vendor-provided models. If you are considering doing so as a shortcut, please think twice. Using these types of models as a review of your Enterprise Architecture Models is of only limited value, at best. *You* have to *do* the work!

Question: **Why are some government organizations investing heavily in Enterprise Architecture?**

Answer: Some government agencies believe that the industrial age is ending and that the information age is gaining momentum, so they want to reskill their people to address what they see as the new economy. Other government agencies are investing in Enterprise Architecture because citizens are increasing demand for government efficiency, integration (including interjurisdictional), accountability, and transparency.

Question: Is one column in The Enterprise Framework more important than another?

Answer: No. Some approaches and tools optimize one column at the expense of another, which is why we suggest not starting the architecture process with a specific Enterprise Architecture tool. All columns are equally important to the enterprise.

Question: Is any column or row in The Enterprise Framework a decomposition or more granular than another column or row?

Answer: No. Decomposition/granularity occurs within each cell (an intersection of a row and column in The Enterprise Framework), and each cell represents the entire organization from the perspective/transformation of that cell. For example, the intersection of the "Define the Business" row and the "Goals" column contains all of the Goals and strategies for the entire organization. Other cells represent different transformations/perspectives.

Question: Where are objects (object orientation) in The Enterprise Framework?

Answer: Objects are implementation composites that contain data and methods, and would be represented as an "Implementation Model" within Enterprise Architecture. The Enterprise Framework represents both Architecture Artifacts and Implementation Artifacts contained within an Enterprise Architecture. There are 30 possible Architecture Models of interest to an enterprise, and 684 (yes!) Implementation Models of interest to an enterprise, contained within The Enterprise Framework. Another common Implementation Model is an Information Model, which defined against the frame of reference—The Enterprise Framework—is the result of combing a model of the data, and a model of the processes.

Question: **Where are web services in The Enterprise Framework?**

Answer: Web services are self-contained applications that perform Processes over the Internet. Some are involved purely with communications, making them "Where" column entities. Others enable business Processes, making them "How" column entities. Also, the related "Software as a Service" is a recent form of entirely hosted Internet applications, which suggests clients could support certain business processes without internal infrastructure. These would be "How" column entries as well.

Question: **Where does Business Process Management fit into The Enterprise Framework?**

Answer: Business Process Management (BPM) is represented at the intersection of the "Business Model" row and the "How" column.

Question: **Where does the Rational Unified Process fit into The Enterprise Framework?**

Answer: Rational Unified Process (RUP) is an iterative software development life cycle (SDLC). So, it fits in the "Technology Neutral" and "Technology Specific" rows.

Glossary of Terms

Affinity: an inherent likeness or set of relationships.

Affinity Analysis: a technique that enables things to be clustered or grouped into related or meaningful categories.

Alignment: cooperation and coordination between components. Enterprise components may need to be adjusted or arranged to optimize alignment.

Anchor object: the architecture component (Goals, Processes, Materials, Roles, Locations, or Events) that the enterprise model analysis is based on. If Processes are selected, as an example, Implementation Models are used to compare the Processes to each of the other components.

Architecture: the art and science of building something, and the manner in which components and artifacts are organized.

Artifact: all structured and unstructured content that describes the what, how, where, who, when, and why of a complex object. Enterprise Architecture artifacts describe the strategies, business drivers, principles, stakeholders, units, locations, budgets, processes, services, information, communications, applications, systems, and infrastructure components.

Associations: describe how Goals, Processes, Materials, Roles, Locations, and Events, and other artifacts of interest, relate to each other. They are the foundation for forming projects.

Baseline Architecture: the series of explicit representations that describe the current enterprise. This becomes the basis for managing change and measuring the effects of change.

Blueprint: a set of models and textual representations that describe the current enterprise, target architecture, or plan.

Business and Technology alignment: references cooperation between Processes to optimize the organization's performance and return on investment.

Business Stakeholders: individuals from the business with hands-on knowledge of the area under analysis.

Consolidation Opportunity: a way to reduce costs by standardizing business processes or systems and eliminating redundancy.

Custodian: Organizational role responsible for the integrity, overall accuracy, currency, consistency, and quality of assigned models and descriptions.

Data Flow Diagram: a graphical representation that describes how data flows between internal or external entities, such as organizations, business Processes, systems, or data stores.

Decomposition Diagram: a hierarchical organization of a component.

Developers: individuals with hands-on technical knowledge of the system under study.

Elevator Pitch: a well-defined project overview that can be delivered in a few minutes, gets the listeners' attention, and lets the listeners know why they should support the project.

Enterprise: a collection of organizations and people with a common set of Goals or single bottom line. An enterprise can be a corporation, business unit, government organization, department, or a network linked together by a common objective.

Enterprise Architecture: explicitly describing an organization through a set of independent, non-redundant artifacts, defining how these artifacts interrelate with each other, and developing a set of prioritized, aligned initiatives and roadmaps to understand the organization, communicate this understanding to stakeholders, and move the organization forward to its desired state.

Enterprise Modeling: activities that identify and define the Goals, business Processes, Materials, Roles, Locations, and Events requirements associated with the business of the organization.

Enterprise Model Analysis: a set of activities that identify the projects required to help the organization achieve its objectives and prioritize implementation projects.

Event: a significant happening that obligates the business area to take action.

Event Partitioned Data Flow Diagram (EPDFD): a rendering that displays precedence order of Processes and the initiating Event(s).

External Agent: a business function, organization, or person that provides or receives information external to the business area.

Framework: a structure that organizes a set of related data or artifacts. The framework shows the relationships between components and brings a totality perspective to otherwise individual components. The framework makes the unorganized organized and coherent. A framework (frame of reference) is the fundamental component required to understand any thing, any profession, or any idea. It is not arbitrary.

Goal: a measurable objective that describes the as is or future vision for the organization and the objectives that the organization's actions must achieve.

Granularity: a measure of the size of the component or level of detail under consideration.

Grass Roots: informal or unsanctioned.

Horse Race: a contest or competition between organizations or projects.

Implementation Model: a two-dimensional representation that identifies relationships between two Enterprise Architecture components or planning objects.

Information: data and Process defined with context.

Information Technology: the systems and associated technologies that are used to automate the collection, movement, transformation, storage, reporting, access, and presentation of data, information, voice, graphics, images, and video objects.

Initial Inventory List: a list used to forecast the duration of the systems inventory task, and provide an initial understanding of the degree of automation in the enterprise. An inaccurate list could result in underestimating the level of effort required.

Integration: bringing two things together that are within the boundaries or scope of the enterprise.

Interface: to bring two things together that are part of two disparate scopes or enterprises.

Interview: a one-on-one meeting that is used to gather information, review drafts, and identify changes.

Location: a site where an organization places people, equipment, Processes, or inventory.

Master Data Management: the organization, business process, system, and technical integration architecture used to create and maintain accurate and consistent views of core business materials, such as Customers, Products, Employees, Suppliers, and Assets.

Material: a building block of common "Business Thing" vocabulary, and the foundation for determining how Processes and systems relate and how they can share data.

Methodology: a set of steps, guidelines, and sequences that convey how to perform tasks and the elements to be used against a framework.

Migrate: to transition the enterprise from one state to another.

Model: a representation that is used to visualize components and relationships between components.

Modeling Approach: the techniques used to build the Enterprise Architecture Models. They include skunk works, interviews, workshops, and surveys.

Non-Disclosure Agreement (NDA): a legal agreement between two or more parties where the parties agree not to share information gained during the engagement with other parties. The agreement should indicate which information cannot be shared (e.g., business strategies, business processes, patents, financial information). The agreement should also indicate how long the information must remain confidential after the agreement terminates. In the case of an Enterprise Architecture planning project, this should be at least three years. This type of agreement may also be called a confidential disclosure agreement (CDA).

Process: an activity performed by the enterprise, with the intent of achieving Goals.

Project: a business improvement project that is scoped during the Enterprise Architecture Model analysis phase, approved during the review and verification phase, and started during the analysis transition phase.

Project Scope: the organization or network that will be impacted by the planning project.

Project Transition Documents: materials that present relevant Enterprise Architecture planning information to the implementation team during the analysis transition phase.

Proof of Concept: a precursor to a full-scale project. It is intended to demonstrate the feasibility of the Enterprise Architecture methodology. A sample or subset of the full Enterprise Architecture activities is used to conduct the proof of concept.

Role: describes how the "who" components of the enterprise are defined and structured. Roles are linked to Processes to illustrate how the enterprise Process skills are executed.

Service Oriented Architecture (SOA): a style of technology intended to facilitate reuse and integration by creating relatively independent software components that can be found and used by other software components. Users of the service are intended to be insulated from implementation details or changes made to the service. The concept is similar to a consumer using a cell phone, television, or web site. SOA may also be referred to as *web services*.

System: an organized and correlated set of components that support one or more of an organization's Processes. An automated system contains a combination of hardware, software, and data communication devices.

Systems Inventory: a system or list that documents details about the systems that have been used to perform and automate Processes. It may also be called a configuration management database, technology asset inventory, business systems inventory, systems inventory, application inventory, or services inventory. It could be implemented as either a centralized or federated repository.

Target/Desired State Architecture: the series of explicit representations that describe the future vision of the enterprise.

Transition Plan: the plans and projects required to transform the enterprise from the baseline architecture—the current state—to the target architecture, the desired state.

Workshop: a structured meeting led by a facilitator. In the Enterprise Architecture Modeling phase, a workshop is used to interactively analyze and represent the enterprise models.

Top Ten Enterprise Architect Certification Program Characteristics Checklist

As the field of Enterprise Architecture (EA) grows and the number of practitioners also increases, the need to distinguish Enterprise Architecture from other professions is greater than ever. Additionally, the need for proper EA training and certification is ever increasing.

Because of these needs, it is not surprising that even in a young field such as Enterprise Architecture, the number of certification programs to choose from is growing. Type "Enterprise Architect Certification" into any search engine and see the vast number of results.

With many Enterprise Architect Certification programs to choose from, picking the right one can be a difficult task. With no set of worldwide recognized standards for EA certification yet available, how do you know you are picking the right one? Which Certification programs will give you the best measures of an architect's capabilities?

We have developed a checklist based on questions that those seeking Enterprise Architect Certification commonly ask. It will enable you to evaluate each Certification program, aid in your selection process, and ensure that the EA Certification program you choose delivers the most practical, effective measure of enterprise architect maturity and capabilities possible.

1. You can actually develop an effective Enterprise Architecture after you finish the certification program

This is the number one criterion for choosing any Enterprise Architect Certification program. A good certification program does not leave its attendees feeling lost once it is over and they are certified. A certified Enterprise Architect should be fully capable, confident, and have a good understanding of how to conduct an architecture project immediately after finishing the program. The program should provide attendees with a toolset (manuals, project plans, templates, etc.) for beginning architecture projects.

A complete Enterprise Architecture Certification program includes:

- An Enterprise Architecture Process

- An Enterprise Architecture classification, taxonomy, and Framework

- An Enterprise Architecture Work Breakdown Structure and Methodology

- An Enterprise Architect Maturity Model

- An Organization Change Model, Process, Methodology, and Work Breakdown Structure

- A set of Business understanding components

- A set of Technology understanding components

- An understanding of Enterprise Architecture Models

- An understanding of Enterprise Solution Models

- Components geared toward "short-term value" that can be built upon to provide "long-term value"

- Templates and tools to provide immediate practitioner guidance

- Criteria to allow practitioners to be recognized for growing competencies as their experience grows, based on actual Enterprise Architecture enablement activities

- Classroom presentation and workshop materials

2. The information has theoretical soundness

Every discipline, whether mathematics, chemistry, or social work, has a theoretical background. Theory is the basis for ideas, techniques, and knowledge methodologies. Therefore, certified Enterprise Architects must study the theory behind the methodologies being taught. Of course, theory alone is not enough for a practitioner. Without a sound understanding of what Enterprise Architecture is and how to move from theory to practice, the true value of EA work will not be achieved. Methodologies taught in EA certification programs should have a traceable theoretical soundness.

3. The courses are based in a defined body of knowledge

To advance the EA profession, a body of knowledge must be defined and the methods taught in the certification program must use it as a reference point. By using a defined body of knowledge, EA results will be consistent and can be verified against it to ensure success. Of course, the body of knowledge will grow over time, and the certification program's theoretical and practicing knowledge base will need to be updated as new understandings are discovered, practiced, and verified.

4. The certifying organization is practitioner-based

The certifying organization should be composed of practitioners— Enterprise Architects who have actually practiced, and continue to practice, Enterprise Architecture. The instructor(s) and advisory Board of Directors should be Enterprise Architects themselves, practicing the same body of knowledge and methodologies taught in the certification program. The practicing Enterprise Architects' understandings will be balanced with the need for theoretical soundness and will maintain that understanding.

5. The courses ask you to demonstrate competency

The certification program should not just be a series of lectures, and competency should not be measured only by success on tests or interviews with experts. The curriculum *should* encourage attendees to practice the theories and methodologies being taught and present opportunities for analysis of demonstrated work in a workshop environment. There is nothing like having to actually do something in front of others to focus your attention! Enterprise Architecture is founded on communicating with a wide array of people in business and IT roles (among many other characteristics), and Enterprise Architecture skills need to be demonstrated. For advanced certification, demonstration of additional Enterprise Architecture work products is necessary to illustrate proficiency. Competency also needs to be recertified periodically, as is the practice in most professions and professional organizations.

6. The instructors are practitioners

Course instructors must be practitioners of Enterprise Architecture themselves, well versed in both the theory and practice of Enterprise Architecture. When they are not teaching, they should be practicing the same body of knowledge being taught in the certification program. Good instructors balance time in the classroom with time doing actual Enterprise Architecture activities within their own enterprises or client enterprises. They are then able to provide a positive learning experience, create an open forum for sharing knowledge, and share personal project experiences with attendees. Preferably, instructors have at least ten years of experience practicing Enterprise Architecture and have had at least twenty-five client/ enterprise engagements.

7. The courses analyze client case studies

The EA certification instructors must be able to offer real examples from real organizations. Attendees want to hear about successful EA projects and pitfalls, not just theoretical examples. Actual stories, quotes, models, and even pictures not only enhance the learning process but also prove to attendees that the defined body of knowledge they will be practicing actually works.

8. The courses teach initiative formation

Enterprise Architecture does not end with a series of models. If it did, then what you would have is a series of models. The Enterprise Architecture methodology taught in a certification program should enable the Enterprise Architect to provide a business or client with an answer to the all-too-familiar question "What am I supposed to do Monday morning?" Simply handing clients a leather-bound book containing a thousand pages of text or a series of models will not allow them to move forward. Appropriately certified Enterprise Architects will be able to deliver a prioritized, business-aligned roadmap—a set of actions or initiatives—of how to proceed from the architecture descriptors.

9. Renewal of certification is available

Most professional certifications are time-limited. Certification means nothing if the last time someone practiced in the field was years ago. As in other professions, Enterprise Architecture certification should be consistent with this concept. Further, as the Certified Enterprise Architect completes architecture projects and demonstrates continued practice in the field, his or her hard work and accomplishments should be recognized through different levels of certification. Advanced certifications, based on the number of actual successful Enterprise Architecture engagements completed, is one measure of meeting advanced certification requirements.

10. The certificate is vendor-neutral

The certifying organization should not accept funding or support from outside sources such as software or service vendors. While software or service vendors are welcome and encouraged to attend certification programs, neutrality is necessary to ensure that all Enterprise Architects practice from the same body of knowledge without bias or outside influence. Professions outside of Enterprise Architecture have maintained this requirement successfully.

This article was prepared by Dana Baer, an EACOE Certified Enterprise Architecture Fellow. She can be reached at <u>Dana.Baer@PinnacleBusGrp.</u> <u>com</u>

On Enterprise Architecture

People interested in Enterprise Architecture are in a difficult spot; we believe it has become more difficult than ever to separate Enterprise Architecture facts from beliefs, experiences from opinions, and sound practices from declarations. The field appears so irregular because consultants, practitioners, academics, and publications present Enterprise Architecture in disparate voices advancing a multitude of approaches, meanings, and sets of expectations—some based on experience, some based on conjecture, and some based on opinion. With blogs, forums, dozens of enterprise architecture organizations of various types, and the Internet itself, how do you sort things out?

- An important first question is, *"Does this make sense?"*

  We try to relate physical analogies to what we hear about Enterprise Architecture. If something does not make sense in the physical world, it probably is not true in the Enterprise or Enterprise Architecture world.

  That is, we suggest that you favor *logic* over what you want to believe.

- Another good question is, *"Is this statement just a bunch of words?"*

  Nothing is true just because it is stated frequently.

- A third question is *"Who is saying this, and what is his or her background?"*

  Has someone who says something about Enterprise Architecture (whatever the definition) verifiably ever done it?

There are many more questions you can think of to test the value of claims. Just be sure to ask them!

To show how lost you can get on Internet Enterprise Architecture forums, for instance, a response to a question where to get Enterprise Architecture information suggests:

> *Do a Google search; there is plenty of information available about Enterprise Architecture. Wikipedia has a concise description of it.*

The response from another forum participant was:

> *This is good advice. Every neurosurgeon, before operating, should quickly do a few Google searches, consult Wikipedia, or pop out and canvass ten or so passers-by in the street to get a "grassroots" feel about thoughts on the latest developments in his/her field!*

We have nothing against Google or Wikipedia (or any other sources of the kind), but—point well taken!

What follows is a compilation of the most common questions from attendees at the Enterprise Architecture Center of Excellence (EACOE) Certification Workshops and our responses. We hope you will find the responses to these questions logical, fact-based, and grounded in sound practices and principles. We can assure you that our responses are definitively based on decades of practice experience and hope that our credentials are meaningful to you.

What **is** Enterprise Architecture?

Enterprise Architecture defined *from an information and technology perspective:*
Enterprise Architecture is explicitly describing an organization through a set of independent, nonredundant artifacts, defining how these artifacts interrelate with each other, and developing a set of prioritized, aligned initiatives and roadmaps to understand the organization, communicate this understanding to stakeholders, and move the organization forward to its desired state.

Enterprise Architecture defined *from a business perspective:*

> Enterprise Architecture illuminates how an organization and all of its members can achieve its objectives through the creation of a series of engineered models and project initiatives that can be easily understood by all of the people associated with the organization.

Within these definitions, how do you define the term "Enterprise"?

A definition of "Enterprise" in this context is any collection of organizations/people and related things that have a common set of goals/principles and/or a single bottom line. Accordingly, an Enterprise can be a whole corporation, a division of a corporation, a government organization, a single department, a project, a team, or a network of geographically distant organizations linked together by common objectives. The wider the definition of the term "enterprise," the more opportunity there is for integration. A narrow definition of enterprise leads to more interfacing.

And within these definitions, how do you define the term "Architecture"?

Architecture is the art and science of representing building (construction) and the manner in which components and artifacts are organized, related, and integrated.

Is Enterprise Architecture about information technology (IT) or is it about the entire enterprise?

It is not a question of mutual exclusivity (one *or* the other). Enterprise Architecture is about *both* the enterprise (business understanding) and the technology enablement (IT) of the enterprise. The definition of Enterprise Architecture above shows this. By the way, "technology" can mean something as simple as pencil and paper.

This question leads to another: "What does the Enterprise Architect do?"

Many mistakenly believe that the Enterprise Architect does *everything* in the field of Enterprise Architecture. But doctors do not do everything in the medical profession, electrical engineers do not do everything in the engineering profession, and so on. The EACOE defined twelve mutually exclusive Architecture Modeling Roles, providing clear and complete role responsibility. There are no loose ends or unassigned gray areas to be overlooked, or to be a source of concern, in Enterprise Architecture. The roles are: Enterprise Architect, Business Architect, Process Architect, Data Architect, Policy/Rule Architect, Role Architect, Logistic Architect, Event/Sequence Architect, Rule Assertion Architect, Workflow Architect, Technology Architect, and Event State Architect. Of course, to deploy all of these roles efficiently and effectively, they must be governed by a clear frame of reference.

I guess I do enterprise information technology architecture, then...that's good, isn't it?

We're not really sure what the phrase "enterprise information technology architecture" means. If it means the current layout and inventory of technology assets, then it should be called *technology assets and logistics layout.* If it means the connectivity of various technology assets, it can be called the *technology blueprint.*

Architecture and implementation are different. You may be able to "architect" the current assets of information technology, but without the Enterprise Architecture desired state, architecting the desired-state technology architecture has little value (we did not say it has *no* value!).

You need to ask some questions: What are you architecting against? How do you know if the technology has anything to do with the business and its future intent? Referring back to the definition of Enterprise Architecture, you'll see that it is about understanding the business intent and the technology to achieve it. Setting up an enterprise information technology architecture out of context from the Enterprise Architecture is not advisable. Organizations doing so may be a reason why people believe that Enterprise Architecture is about information technology only.

There are many frameworks out there, so I can use any one of them, right?

A framework is a structure that organizes a set of related artifacts. The framework shows the relationships of the artifacts of the chosen subject area and brings a totality perspective to otherwise individual ideas. A framework, therefore, makes the unorganized organized and coherent, and it is fundamental to any profession or discipline (engineering, chemistry, physics, language, music—anything). Framework elements must be mutually exclusive and collectively exhaustive.

A framework that is in constant update and versioning is troubling. If it is, it is not (or was not) complete. If we were using Version 4 of the framework and we now have Version 9, what does that say about the work we did with Version 4? Can you imagine the English alphabet starting off with fifteen letters (Version 1), then going to twenty-one (Version 2), and then twenty-six (version 3), with more proposed versions yet to come? How useful would that be? Can you imagine the periodic table of chemical elements having multiple versions? Chemistry would be like alchemy. Can you imagine the system of musical notes to be in continuous versioning? (It would really fun to play in an orchestra.) A framework is fundamental to Enterprise Architecture. The Enterprise Framework™ and the framework defined by John Zachman meet the criteria for an Enterprise Architecture framework.

And "methodology"? That's just another word for "framework," right?

No. A framework is not a methodology, and a methodology is not a framework. A framework can possibly accommodate many methodologies, but we have not seen a methodology work across multiple frameworks (at least not in the physical world. We can't see how it could be different in the Enterprise Architecture world). A methodology is a set of practices and procedures applied to a specific branch of knowledge. A methodology contains proven processes to follow in planning, defining, analyzing, designing, building, testing, and implementing the area under consideration. An outstanding methodology guides, simplifies, and standardizes the process; it can be customized to meet an organization's specific standards and practices. An outstanding methodology is correct, up to date, complete, and concise; it defines deliverables; it has methods, techniques, standards, practices, roles and responsibilities; it has suggested timings and sequences and dependencies; and it has associated education.

Guidelines are not methodologies either. A guideline might tell you what operations you can do or provide suggestions on deliverables. Methodologies should provide a predefined *path* or paths. A methodology should allow you to *do* something "Monday morning"—you shouldn't have to figure out how to take a guideline and turn it into a path. The Pinnacle Business Group, Inc. Quick Start Methodology meets the criteria for an Enterprise Architecture Methodology.

I need my Enterprise Architecture to fit on one page. After all, it only has to be at a high level.

We are not sure why it's important to stay within one page, but whatever you're trying to do, it is not an Enterprise Architecture. If you have ever had the privilege (or frustration) of building a house, you know you get a "scroll" of diagrams (blueprints) for the house. If something as simple as a house needs a scroll of drawings, an Enterprise Architecture will also require at least one.

This analogy suggests another hint: There is no one "picture" in the set of house blueprints that solves all constituents' or stakeholders' needs. Similarly, no single drawing or representation solves all needs for all Enterprise Architecture stakeholders: the complexity is much greater. Different audiences require different criteria. (Our primary criterion for business-facing models is whether they are "human-consumable." Our primary criterion for technology- and implementation-facing models is whether they are transformable into solutions.)

We suggest that there are thirty possible Architectural Model representations and 684 possible Implementation Model representations that may be of interest to segments of enterprise stakeholders. We can calculate this census of models because we have a frame of reference. We don't have to develop *all* of these representations—just the ones that we decide are relevant. However, just because something is not made explicit does not mean it does not exist; it is just implicit. But in not making something explicit, we are making a value judgment. We are very glad that we can understand what we know and are making explicit, but we also know what we are making assumptions about (what remains implicit) when we have the Framework acting as our frame of reference.

Enterprises aren't like physical items. They don't need the level of specificity of buildings or airplanes or ocean liners, right?

In two words: why not? We don't know why people believe this.

We believe that enterprises are actually much *more* complex than any of these physical items. If you are building a rowboat, you probably do not need much architecture. If you are building an ocean liner, you need extensive architecture, and at great detail. If you are building a model airplane, you probably do not need much architecture. If you are building a *Boeing* 747 that flies over water at night (with us in it!), you need extensive architecture. Compare, too, a log cabin to a one-hundred-story building. Ask the people who completed the Trump International Hotel and Tower in Chicago how much time they spent on architecture and how much they spent on implementation. You might be surprised. But we don't think you will be surprised at the level of detail in the buildings' architecture.

If you are building a worldwide enterprise that has thousands of employees and is undergoing constant change, you need extensive architecture. Architecture is the baseline for managing complexity and change. Without it, what will you use to address complexity and change, and what are you going to do to avoid unintended consequences (that is, you had no details in your architecture)? Architecture is about planning, analyzing, designing, and constructing. We wish enterprises would stop using the prevalent life cycle: constructing, maintaining, maintaining, maintaining. What is your approach to managing complexity and change if it isn't Enterprise Architecture?

We aren't saying that you have to do everything at once. Enterprise Architecture is a continuous process with greater granularity of its artifacts over time as the enterprise changes and as more of the enterprise is mechanized or automated. Architecture occurs prior to making a change. Documentation occurs after the change is made. This is the only logical, practical, and cost-effective way to proceed. Our objective is to continually reduce the risk of unintended consequences and inappropriate changes.

What abilities are required to implement Enterprise Architecture?

The skills mix for the twelve Roles defined for Enterprise Architecture changes according to their levels within The Enterprise Framework. We suggest that both hard and soft abilities and skills are required to different degrees for all Architect Roles in an Enterprise Architecture, but generally, more soft skills (facilitation, meeting dynamics, communications, etc.) are required at the business-layer roles than at the other layers. More hard skills (modeling, technology transformations, etc.) are required at the technology-transformation layers of the Framework.

You often analogize Engineering and Manufacturing. Why?

We do not know if we will ever truly be able to engineer and/or manufacture an enterprise, but we see how the two domains are analogous. We recognize a common path of development from handcrafting things to engineering things in almost every discipline that we can think of.

New disciplines tend to begin with manufacturing (Implementation), such as the handcrafting of automobiles a hundred-fifty years ago. Once there is a codified body of knowledge (engineering) about a discipline, it is used to produce better-engineered products (better implementations). So, the sequence is: manufacturing to engineering to better-manufactured products. The way enterprises work is analogous. Most of what is done in enterprises can be thought of as Implementation (manufacturing). We are now codifying this enterprise understanding as Architecture (engineering), and eventually we will be able to produce better enterprise Implementations. In other words, the analogous sequence in enterprises will be implementations to architecture to better-implemented solutions and products.

What is the Business Application Information Technology (BAIT) model for Enterprise Architecture?

The BAIT model was one early attempt to define what models are required for Enterprise Architecture. It was developed with systems implementations as the primary target and was not based on a frame of reference (a Framework). Its most strident previous supporters now call this an "IT stack." and we agree that this positioning makes more sense.

Figures

Samuel B. Holcman
Biography

SAMUEL B. (Sam) HOLCMAN is the Chairman of the Pinnacle Business Group, Inc., the President of the Zachman Institute for Framework Advancement (ZIFA), and the Managing Director of the Enterprise Architecture Center Of Excellence (EACOE), and the Business Architecture Center Of Excellence (BACOE). He is considered the practitioners practitioner in Enterprise Architecture and Business Architecture, and the leading implementer and world-wide educator and trainer in Enterprise Architecture and Business Architecture methodologies and techniques.

The Pinnacle Business Group, Inc. and its associated organizations provide its clients with innovative, yet practical solutions to a range of business and systems related challenges and activities. He was the Vice President of Modelware, Methodologies, and BPE (Business Process Engineering) for a major software company. Prior to this experience, Mr. Holcman was the Founder and President of Computer and Engineering Consultants, Ltd. His interests include consulting and research on topics such as enterprise architecture, business architecture, business process engineering, intellectual capital management, organization development, system methodologies and life cycles, corporate business modeling, and accelerated analysis techniques. Mr. Holcman conceptualized and constructed a unique look at system development methodologies, which resulted in the highly regarded ForeSight ™ methodology and methodology management product.

He has developed a strategic planning process that is used by many Fortune 500 companies, and is the co-developer of the widely used accelerated analysis (JAD-like) technique known as Rapid Analysis. He has also developed an innovative approach to Business Process Re-Engineering known as Business Process Visualization ™ and Organization Network

Analysis ™. These techniques are being used to Unlock the Hidden Assets in your Organization ℠.

In association with Mr. John A. Zachman, he formed The Zachman Institute for Framework Advancement (ZIFA), to explore, explain, and share the concepts of enterprise architecture. Sam has been focusing on understanding the value and management of Intellectual Capital to enterprises. He has developed the Intellectual Capital Maturity Model ™ to provide guidance on how effectively organizations are managing their Intellectual Capital, and steps they can take to more effectively manage this capital, and the Enterprise Architecture Maturity Model, to provide guidance to organizations seeking to improve their understanding and implementation of Enterprise Architecture concepts. He has developed and published works on Cooperatively Optimized Relationships (COR), which is the next generation of understandings in the field of Customer Relationship Management (CRM). To better understand an organizations "DNA", Sam led the development of The Enterprise Framework ™ and The Business Architecture Framework ™. Both The Enterprise Framework, and The Business Architecture Framework have received worldwide acclaim for their understandability, and usability, while maintaining theoretical purity.

Sam was with Ford Motor Company for 11 years in data processing, finance, and engineering. He was Vice President of a robotics and factory automation firm for two years. He was also a senior member of a technology delegation to the People's Republic of China, on the invitation of the Chinese and United States Government, and a member of a technology delegation to the Commonwealth of Independent States (Soviet Union).

Sam has a Bachelor's degree in Bioengineering and Master's Degree in Electrical Engineering from Wayne State University in Detroit, Michigan, and a Master's in Business Administration from the University of Michigan, Ann Arbor. He has been elected to Eta Kappa Nu (electrical engineering honors society), and Tau Beta Pi (engineering honors society), and is a member of numerous societies and professional organizations, and is a frequent speaker at seminars around the world. He can be emailed at Samuel.Holcman@PinnacleBusGrp.com, or reached by telephone on (810) 231-0531.

References

1   *Governing IT in the Enterprise* (Forrester Research, Inc., July 30, 2004).

2   *The House Science Subcommittee on Basic Research Hearing on IT for the 21st Century* (March 16, 1999).

3   Gilbert Alorie, "Bush budget proposes hefty IT increase," CnetNews. com (Mar 9, 2002).

4   E-Government Act of 2002 (H.R. 2458), Pub. L. No. 107-347 (2002).

7   *Flip the Ratio–Decrease IT Maintenance, Increase IT Innovation*, Hewlett-Packard Development Company, L.P., (2006).

8   Mike Hales, Julie Metelko, and Frank Fehrenbach, *Spending Smarter: Rebalancing the IT Budget* (A.T. Kearney, 2005).

Made in the USA
Middletown, DE
10 October 2016